MOVING TO COSTA RICA
SIMPLIFIED

NOT YOUR TYPICAL
EXPAT GUIDE

from award-winning author
Chrissy Gruninger

A *for Harmony* Publication © 2024

All Rights Reserved.

This book, or parts thereof, may not be reproduced in any form without permission of the author.

Cover design by Mau Villalobos Diseño Gráfico, maureenvillalobos.com

The information provided in this book is created with the intention of offering useful content to the reader. The author has done her best to provide accurate and up-to-date information, however errors can occur, and relevant laws and regulations can change.

The author is not liable for any possible inaccuracies or omissions, nor for any consequences that may arise because of using this information. It is not intended as legal, financial, therapeutic, medical, or professional advice, and should not be construed as such. The reader assumes full responsibility for the use of the information provided.

Readers are advised to seek professional advice when necessary and to conduct their own due diligence to verify any information upon which they intend to rely.

Use of this content signifies your acceptance of these terms.

Also by Chrissy Gruninger

The Rich Coast Collection

Vicarious Adventures on the Rich Coast
No Fear
Lost and Found in the Land of Mañana
Moving to Costa Rica Simplified

Living Well Collection

There's Always Something
Wildhearted Cooking
Meet Me in the Middle
A Wildhearted Sanguine Life
An Intentional Life
An Interconnected Life
A Harmonious Life
Nourishing Wisdom
Living Intentionally
Daily Yoga

CONTENTS

Ch 1: Leaping & Letting Go 1
Ch 2: A Little Detour 7
Ch 3: Your First Steps 10
Ch 4: Moving Forward, *Not* Escaping 15
Ch 5: Is Costa Rica Expensive? 19
Ch 6: Location Location Location 24
Ch 7: A Place to Call Home 34
Ch 8: Buying vs Renting 43
Ch 9: Buying 49
Ch 10: Building 54
Ch 11: Renting 63
Ch 12: Mother Nature 67
Ch 13: Moving with Children 81
Ch 14: Moving with Pets 88
Ch 15: Residency 93
Ch 16: Healthcare 105
Ch 17: Banking & Money Matters 130
Ch 18: Cultural Awareness & Adjustment 141
Ch 19: The Expat Experience 153
Ch 20: Mental Health 164
Ch 21: Personal Relations 173
Ch 22: Language Tips 180
Ch 23: Expressions 186
Ch 24: Fun. Interesting. Random 192
Ch 25: Legal Matters 202
Ch 26: The Government 205
Ch 27: Holidays & Observances 216
Ch 28: Driving, Road Rules & Safety 223
Ch 29: In Case of Emergency 235

Ch 30: Welcome to the Jungle...........................240
Ch 31: Shopping..245
Ch 32: Shipping...250
Ch 33: The Dark Side of Paradise......................254
Ch 34: Be a Good Expat...................................286
Ch 35: Suffrage & Beyond................................309
Ch 36: Do You Have a Plan B?.........................335
Ch 37: Reflections..337

DEDICATION

To you, my dear reader.

May you make your dream a reality.

Preface

Hola y bienvenid@*! Thank you for choosing this not-so-typical expat guide on how to move to, and live in, Costa Rica, the country I've called home since 2012. I'm so happy you're here.

Let me start off by saying... congratulations! It's a big leap you're taking, and one very few people do in their lifetime.

And if you're already living here but looking for a tad extra support, *¡Felicidades!*

Let's get a little housekeeping out of the way before we jump in.

Be sure to read this book in its entirety. While there are no guarantees, this book was designed to help you with a successful and sustainable transition to living abroad in Costa Rica.

What do I mean by that?

I want to see you thrive. I want to see you move here, put down roots and *really* love your life on the Rich Coast.

*You'll learn why I use the @ symbol in the Suffrage & Beyond chapter!

When I say "sustainable", while that usually (*in my world*) has some kind of eco-friendly meaning... this time around, it actually means long-term. Or for however long you hope to call Costa Rica home. Whether you're only planning on staying here a year or it becomes your forever home, this book is for you.

I've written this book in such a way that it shouldn't need to be updated regularly. I don't want you to have to buy a new book every year. However, there are some chapters when I talk about laws and procedures and in those sections, you'll see the year that I'm publishing this – 2024. Please know that those sections might change. The government here often moves at a sloth's pace, but change does eventually happen. I'll update the book when there are big changes and I'll do my best to keep you posted on social media, my website and inside my email community.

I'm from the United States originally so a lot of the examples in this book will reference the US. While I always want to have an expanded worldview and be aware of what's happening in different parts of the planet, it would be inappropriate to give examples from other countries. I also use colones or US dollars when writing about money.

I give very few references in this book. Businesses here open and close like the sun rises and sets. You can recommend an individual or business one day and then tomorrow find out that they stole from someone, they took two months to do something that should have taken a day, they gave bad advice, or they did any other number of unethical things.

In my work with private clients, I do offer referrals as that is *in the moment* and I can confidently make a recommendation and ensure the contractor follows through. In a book, not so much. Also to note, I don't take commissions from those I refer. Costa Rica thrives on kickbacks but I'd rather the client get a reduced (or at least *fair*) fee than pocket the money for myself. And if I ever did get a commission or kickback, I would disclose it upfront. #*integritymatters*

As you read this book, you'll see... I'm very much a realist, you'll get no superficial fluff from me! We'll be taking a deep dive inside this book because knowledge will empower you to make decisions about your move with confidence. It may also highlight questions you didn't even know to ask.

Inside I'll share with you both the amazing and the not-so-ideal. You might not always like what I write in the book. I encourage you to approach each challenge that I present with a curious mind.

There are some serious discussions to be had and I'd rather you know now, before you move, than be surprised when you arrive. Understanding the reality will help you manage your expectations so you can make an informed decision of *whether or not Costa Rica is right for you*... and that's one of the many objectives I hope to support you with, inside this book.

What's Inside

This book was gigantic when it all came together!

While my goal with this book is to simplify the process of moving to Costa Rica, I realized too much information would be really overwhelming. The last thing I want to do is stress you out.

Think of this book like a GPS that guides you easily to your destination, showing you not only the amazing places to explore and discover, but also the roadblocks and detours to expect along the way.

I kept all the information you need to know, while removing some of the less essential details. You'll see simplified *snapshot* sections throughout the book, to help you reflect and figure out what next steps you should take.

And like I said above, for some topics, we're going deep, because even though I've simplified it, that doesn't mean we don't have a whole lot of important material to cover.

This book is also a massive detour for me from the types of books I normally write that are all about stories, experiences, and prose. *But I couldn't not include any...* so you'll see some of those sprinkled throughout the book.

Inside you'll find helpful information, essays, and simplified snapshots of the many considerations you should be aware of... from a (*mostly*) unbiased perspective in order to help you figure out if Costa Rica is right for you and prep you to take the leap.

The unbiased perspectives are important in this book (*in comparison to other books I've written*) because we all come here from different backgrounds, with different beliefs and I'd rather not alienate those of you who think differently from me. As much as possible, I believe in trying to meet people in the middle rather than digging our heels in on opposite sides.

That said, I'll *occasionally* give my own personal opinion and experiences as well as the experiences of people that I've worked with and met along the way.

The stories and challenges shared are meant to give you a glimpse into what to expect, however it doesn't mean it will happen to *you*. Think of them like cautionary tales to help guide you in your move abroad.

Knowing what to expect can also make life *simpler*! It's like having the quiz answers in advance. This is truly the book I wish I had when I moved here; fewer mistakes would have been made.

Love pros and cons lists? They're included as well. I wanted to do as much of the legwork for you, so that as much as possible, you only have to go to one resource to find the information you're looking for.

And as promised, I'm sharing with you two gifts to help you prepare. You can download them here: www.costaricaexpatexpert.com/simplified

If you don't agree with everything I write, *that's okay*. Keep an open mind, and if something doesn't resonate with you, then as my friend julia butterfly hill says, "toss it in the compost", give it a twirl and move on to the next section.

If you feel like personalized support would be helpful in your move abroad, know that I'm here for you. I work privately with clients as both a relocation counselor, *before you move*, and as a life abroad mentor *once you've arrived*.

Personal Note

Dear reader, this is my 14th book published but my first book since becoming disabled after surviving severe sepsis. Learning a "new normal" has taken its toll on me, my body *and more importantly as it pertains to this book*, my brain.

A few years ago, as I was trying to figure out how to continue earning money while managing my new health challenges, I decided to turn my hobby of relocation counseling into my full-time business. Because I can easily talk about Costa Rica until the cows come home (*well, with some limitations these days, but you get the point!*).

So, I started joining Facebook groups about moving to Costa Rica. I saw how people were not only so awful to one another but also noticed all the misinformation being shared, spreading like invasive, out-of-control weeds.

I knew I needed to get this book into the hands of those of you who maybe couldn't work with me privately but wanted to prepare and know what to expect when moving to Costa Rica. Without harassment or distorted fiction posing as facts.

I worked on this book little by little, day by day, and stayed focused on what brings me joy: writing, sharing stories, and supporting others in making their dreams a reality.

Hiring an editor wasn't an option this time around as I can only work a few hours a week and all my income goes to daily expenses and medical care. I ask you please for your patience and grace.

I have done my absolute best to ensure this book is typo-free, but a few words and grammatical errors may have slipped past me. My brain just doesn't work the way it used to! It literally doesn't see written words in the same way anymore. As someone who loves to write, this has been a difficult, and disheartening, adjustment.

If you see something awry or feel like something is missing, I invite you to reach out to me personally. My contact information is in the back of the book. I'd love to hear from you, even if it's constructive feedback. Leaving a negative review is really so harmful to us indie authors.

Plus, since you've supported my work and livelihood by purchasing this book, I hope that as you read it, you'll feel like you have a friend here on the Rich Coast who is cheering you on.

Thank you again for picking up a copy of this book and supporting my livelihood and small business. I hope you find it helpful in your journey of moving to Costa Rica.

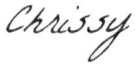

1

Leaping & Letting Go

You've decided to take the leap and move to a new country, possibly a new language, new culture, new laws...

You may feel the fluttering of butterflies in your stomach and your heart may skip a beat in anticipation of all that's to come, but moving abroad, for many, can also feel overwhelming and stressful. *That's totally normal.*

You may have spent decades living in your home country, accumulating a mountain of personal stuff, having a solid set of friends and family nearby, knowing how to pay your electricity bill, property taxes and where to get the best meal when you don't feel like cooking.

For a lot of us, moving to Costa Rica might feel like we've been standing on solid ground for most of our lives and when we disembark the plane, the ground underneath has become quicksand and we're searching for a rope to hold onto.

Let's take a deep breath here. This book will not only act as that rope, but it'll also give you the motivation and momentum to help you manage whatever challenges you face.

Acknowledging that things will be different, and that you won't know everything from the get-go, will help you remember to put one foot in front of the other and to take small steps when things feel tough.

Here's something else to remember: *You can do this.*

Let me tell you a little secret...

One of the best ways you can prepare yourself to move abroad is to recognize that you'll no longer be in control.

You'll be entering a completely different territory. It's a brave new world!

There will (*likely*) be challenges like you've never experienced. There's no getting around that unless you choose to live in a bubble (*which I don't recommend*) and even then, eventually, that bubble will burst.

There's only so long you can hold onto your old ways of thinking, doing, and being before you realize that some changes have to be made.

There may be times when you feel like you're going to need a (*preferably recycled*) paper bag to breathe into. Remembering to breathe – long, deep belly breaths – is imperative!

Is Costa Rica right for you?

That's a serious question I want you to ask yourself as you dive headfirst into this book.

We often think about Costa Rica as this picture-perfect paradise only to realize once we've arrived that maybe it has a few faults, here and there.

My journey to Costa Rica was met with cautionary advice from local friends: *living here is vastly different from a vacation.*

Understanding the potential challenges and difficulties beforehand can significantly improve your transition to living abroad.

A commonly shared statistic among expat groups suggests that most people who relocate here end up leaving within two years.

There is no real data to support that stat but based on what I've seen and the people I've met along the way, it's more or less accurate. About half of the people I've met here moved back after two years or less. But that also means about half of the people I've met are still here.

Costa Rica isn't for everyone. And there are lots of reasons people move back to their home countries or move on to another country. Here's a *snapshot*:

- Medical issues
- Missing family and friends
- Marriage difficulties
- Financial difficulties
- They couldn't adjust to the cultural changes
- Language barriers
- Kids can get a better education elsewhere
- Identity crisis
- Discrimination and prejudice
- Crime
- They thought Costa Rica would fix the problems they were trying to escape from
- Some people even return home because they realized that their home country wasn't all that bad. They learned to appreciate the conveniences that some people find lacking here.

This book will help you prepare so that you can make an informed decision.

So where do we begin?

While not everyone agrees with me, I believe that moving out of your home country, especially to one with a very different culture and language, is a MAJOR life change. Similar to getting married, having a child or getting divorced.

You're about to uproot your entire life, leave behind everything you've ever known and embark on a journey with unexpected surprises... some good, some not-so-ideal.

Stats I found indicate that only 3.5% of the world's population moves out of their home country.

So, begin by giving yourself some kudos... You are truly one in a million! (*Don't do the math on that, it's likely not accurate*).

I'm going to reiterate here... as you prepare for this new adventure, remember that living here is *very* different from being on vacation here. Taking a vacation provides you with a surface level experience where everything is amazing, beautiful and full of *Pura Vida*!

Living here, you may find it's not quite the same. There may be some beliefs and ways of being that you'll need to let go of. Everyone's circumstances are different, and no one will share the exact same journey.

For me, as I share in the book about my personal experiences of moving to Costa Rica, those first few years of living here were a combination of Mr. Toad's Wild Ride, Bonanza and Mad Men.

I published that book in 2017 and a lot has happened since. Once again, some good, some not-so-ideal. A lot of lessons learned. But I'm still here, in this adopted country I call home.

This is what I want for you. To be able to get over the speed bumps, the potholes, the adjustments that you'll likely come across in your everyday life here. To understand what to expect and be prepared for whatever comes your way. In doing so, we simplify the complex and illuminate the unknown so that you can thrive here on the Rich Coast.

2

A Little Detour

We're going to take one little detour before diving in... *thanks for your patience with me.*

Throughout this book, you'll find that I share a lot of stories about the country in general, as well as both foreigners and expats. As a most basic example, I may write something like:

Some Costa Ricans like basketball.

See how I used the word "*some*"? That's a key reminder that I'm not saying ALL locals (or foreigners) think, speak or do something in the same way.

This is important, my friends. It may seem out of place, but you'll see that I refer back to this section repeatedly throughout the book. Don't skip this part!

I see this problem so much in Facebook groups, where people are so convinced that it's always one way or another. Everything is perfect or everything is bleak. *It happens a lot, right?*

Take for example, a discussion around living in Jacó. There will be hundreds of comments about how it's a cesspool of prostitution and drugs. Usually from people who don't actually live there.

People appear so confident in their responses that you wouldn't think twice that maybe the information provided isn't accurate. It can be hard to discern what's fact from fiction.

Yet I know people who live in Jacó and love it... and they're not into the party lifestyle, prostitution or drugs. They live what most people would consider a normal life. Taking their kids to school, working, grabbing a bite to eat, hanging out at the beach to watch the sunset.

Most issues aren't as simple as "all or none," "black or white." There's a whole lot of colorful options in between. Yet, when we get caught up in the heat of the moment, it's easy to forget that.

Black-and-white thinking might feel *comforting* because it gives us a sense of certainty.

Sure, it can make decisions seem simpler—you're either in or you're out, it's either good or bad. *But real talk,* life is rarely that straightforward. It's like having a roadmap with only two directions:

left or right. But the reality is, life's more like a maze with endless twists and turns. Especially for some of us who live in Costa Rica.

When we see things in absolutes, not only are we oversimplifying; we're also shutting down the conversation. Instead of exploring different perspectives, we're too busy digging our heels into our own positions or believing half-truths instead of seeing the bigger picture. And that's where things start to get messy.

An invitation

So, how do we break free from the "all or none" trap? It starts with realizing that life isn't just black and white, rather it's a whole rainbow of possibilities. It means being okay with uncertainty and complexity. It means being open to the idea that maybe, *just maybe*, there's more than one way to look at things.

That's what I'm going to ask you to do inside this book and as you prepare to move and settle here.

Okay, with that out of the way, let's get started on making your dream of moving to Costa Rica a real-life reality.

3

Your First Steps

Why are you choosing to move to Costa Rica? A simpler, slower, and (*possibly*) more affordable lifestyle? To explore a new country? Or something else? Here's a few other reasons people often share...

Costa Rica has become a popular destination for moving abroad, not only those coming from the US, but people all around the world who are seeking an exit to the rat race, in order to live a slower pace of life.

With no military, this is one of the big factors that sets Costa Rica apart from its neighbors in Central America.

Technically, funds were supposed to be redirected to education, healthcare, the environment, and other social welfare programs. We'll explore those ideas more, throughout the book.

And, in comparison to some of its nearby neighbors, the stability of the government here is generally better, although not without its faults. Political stability is closely linked to economic stability.

Expats also choose Costa Rica because, depending on where you're moving from and where you choose to live here, it may be more affordable.

You can enjoy a comfortable standard of living without breaking the bank in many areas around the country. That said, some things are much more expensive here than they are in other countries, and assessing your budget is a must-do before moving.

Many people also move here because of the country's commitment to the environment. This was a big one for me, personally.

The country generates 99% of its electricity from renewable sources, and more than a quarter of its land is protected as national parks or reserves. You do have to be wary however of greenwashing. Just like anywhere else, it happens here, too.

Your next step, before we get too far into this book, is to complete a little homework... *I want you to start thinking about your life here.* Don't worry if you're not totally sure of all the answers, we'll discuss these questions in more detail throughout the book.

So, grab a journal, your favorite beverage and mindfully answer the following questions.

Why Costa Rica? What makes *you* want to call this country, "home"? Is it the climate, culture, cost of living, way of living, business opportunities, or something else? Write them down. Knowing your WHY is imperative and will come in handy *if and when* life starts to go awry.

Have you visited before? Have you spent enough time in Costa Rica to *really* understand its culture, lifestyle, and potential challenges?

Can you afford to live here? Have you looked at your budget, including housing, food, healthcare, vehicle fees, insurance and other expenses?

What's your financial plan? Are you retired with a secure pension? Do you plan to open a business? Work remotely?

Do you speak Spanish? While English is spoken by *some* locals, and there are a lot of English-speaking expats, speaking Spanish can go a long way in helping you integrate.

Will you become a resident and which residency category do you fit into? Investor, retiree, "renter" (working but outside of the country), digital nomad (which is not long-term)?

What will you do for healthcare? You'll likely want adequate coverage or access to medical services, especially if you have ongoing health problems to manage.

Ready for the weather? While most people only think of Costa Rica as a tropical location, it can get cold in some areas. Are you also prepared for the heat, humidity, and rainy season?

What about cultural differences? Are you ready to adapt to a new way of life? *(Many people emphatically say yes before realizing what that means, make sure to read this entire book!)*

How will you manage feeling homesick? Moving to a new country can be challenging emotionally. Have you thought about what it'll be like to live so far away from your family and friends and how you'll deal with that?

What is your goal with moving here? Are you moving to Costa Rica temporarily or permanently? Will you return to your home country in the future? What's your Plan B if this move doesn't work out?

Have you looked into the legal and tax implications? Talk with an accountant in your home country before moving to understand what the tax implications are when living abroad. Understand visas (the stamp in your passport for most foreigners), and residency laws.

What will you do for transportation? Will you ship or drive your vehicle, buy a vehicle here or rely on private or public transportation? What are the transportation options available in the town you plan to live in?

How will you manage your finances? Think about how you will access your money, whether through local banks, international transfers, or other means.

Are you prepared for unexpected challenges? Surprises and obstacles are common here. Are you flexible and resilient enough to manage them?

Are you mentally prepared? Are you ready to embrace the unknown? What fears or hesitations do you have about moving, and how can you overcome them? What excites you the most about this move, and what are you willing to risk?

4

Moving Forward, **_Not_** Escaping

Real Talk... Are you running to Costa Rica or running away from something in your home country?

To clarify, I'm not referring to those individuals who are seeking asylum from a harmful and oppressive regime. Costa Rica is one of the countries that does indeed take in refugees and provides them with legal residency.

But there are a lot of individuals who flee to Costa Rica for other reasons, only to find out that what they were fleeing from, they found once again here on the Rich Coast. Only now, they have no rights, no option to vote and very few ways to make a difference.

I get it. There comes a time in our lives when we feel the urge to change our surroundings, to explore the many possibilities that lie out on the horizon. Sometimes, it's because we need to escape, to flee from challenges or discontent in our current situation. However, it's important to choose a new destination **not as an escape route** but as a leap toward growth and opportunity.

I'm going to stress that _moving from a position of possibility rather than desperation is imperative to make_ when moving to Costa Rica.

Seeking a fresh start? I get that too.

Moving to Costa Rica should be seen as a proactive step towards personal development and transformation, *whatever that looks like for you.*

Rather than fleeing from challenges, it's about accepting the unknown and stepping out of your comfort zone. This shift in perspective transforms the act of moving from a <u>reactive</u> response to circumstances into an <u>intentional</u> choice to create a better future.

A risk of moving to a new country out of desperation is the danger of bringing unresolved problems along with you.

Whether it's financial struggles, relationship problems, political issues, or personal demons, these challenges have a way of resurfacing unless addressed directly. (*We'll talk more about that in the mental health chapter.*)

Moving Forward, Not Escaping

Maybe most importantly, moving to Costa Rica as a means of escape may lead to unrealistic expectations and a sense of disillusionment.

The idea of starting fresh in a tropical paradise can be tempting, but it's essential to recognize that life in Costa Rica, *like anywhere else*, comes with its own set of challenges.

Running away might give you a breather, a little temporary relief, but those problems you left behind... they're still there, simmering away, just waiting for the perfect moment to come back and haunt you.

And guess what? While you're busy managing them, life's throwing a whole new – *and often unexpected* – set of curveballs your way.

Think of it like those pesky weeds in your garden - you pluck one out, and before you know it, a whole new batch sprouts up. Especially here in Costa Rica where weeds grow a foot overnight and multiply like rabbits.

Without careful consideration and preparation, the move can quickly become overwhelming. Adjusting to life in a new country requires more than just a change of scenery; it demands a strategic approach, *which hopefully this book will help you with some of that!*

Please approach this move with realistic expectations and a willingness to confront obstacles head-on.

So let me ask you... are you ready to embrace:

- Change?
- The unknown?
- And the endless possibilities that await you on the Rich Coast?

By approaching the move with intentionality, a curious mind and an open heart, you can create for yourself a beautiful life, where every sunrise brings not just the promise of a new day but the assurance that you are exactly where you're meant to be: living life to the fullest in the land of what many of us get to call our adopted country, Costa Rica.

5

Is Costa Rica Expensive?

Question to ask yourself: *If you're on a budget, can you live a typical lifestyle here and let go of some of the amenities and luxuries you might be used to in your home country? And do you understand what that <u>really</u> means?*

We'll explore the following topics in a lot more detail but since this is always one of the most common questions people ask, I wanted to give you a snapshot in the beginning, so you can start to think about your finances and budget accordingly.

Housing: Cost really depends on the location and what amenities you need. Can you live in a very simple house with just the basics? Or do you need a dryer, dishwasher, bathtub, full size oven and other luxury amenities that aren't common here in less expensive rentals?

Living at the coast or in the GAM (San José area) will probably cost you more. If you're on a limited budget, you may want to consider more rural areas, outside of the city or on the outskirts of coastal areas. Rental prices vary widely, you can find housing for $500 (*or less*) a month, all the way up to $5,000+!

Healthcare: The country's healthcare system includes both public and private options. Paying for the national insurance program, known as "Caja" (Caja Costarricense de Seguro Social – CCSS), is required (in 2024) for all legal residents with a DIMEX or cédula (*you'll learn about those in the Residency chapter*).

The cost depends on your income and residency category; it could be as little as $30-50 per month or upwards of $400 or more, per month. Paying for Caja means that you have access to public hospitals, clinics, and healthcare services (labs, prescriptions, etc) for free.

Everyday Expenses: Whether groceries, dining out, transportation, and utilities are "expensive" is very much dependent on what you're used to paying in your home country.

I don't eat animals so that means I buy a lot of grains, legumes, veggies and fruit. But my grocery bills are usually around $400/month (I'm including cat food, toilet paper, etc in that dollar amount). And it's just me! The other day, I bought a box of Kleenex, and it cost about $7.00, which was a much higher cost than when I compared it to prices on Amazon.

To get an idea of what grocery store items cost, both Walmart (*visit its Costa Rica site*) and Pricesmart (*our version of Costco*) have websites where you can search for items and see how they compare to what you're paying in your home country.

Farmers' markets tend to be less expensive and are an amazing way to get to know your local farmer and be an active participant in supporting your community.

Dining out depends on where you live and what kinds of restaurants you like to frequent. Going to sodas (*small family-owned restaurants*) will be less expensive than choosing to go to any other type of restaurant. But I get it, sometimes you want Thai, Indian or Italian, it's just going to cost you more!

When I was in the States, I had a healthy balance of going out to eat and making home-cooked meals. But in Costa Rica, I have essentially become a professional home chef. Especially since, while I eat a lot of rice and beans, I really do love all kinds of international flavors.

Transportation: Costs in Costa Rica vary. Do you plan on owning a vehicle? In the area where you plan to live, can you drive a regular sedan, or do you need an SUV with 4x4?

I didn't own a vehicle for the first ten years of living here. I took public transportation at times but relied heavily on private taxis (*piratas*). Owning a car (*for me*), is more expensive than not owning one, once I add up all the fees associated with vehicle ownership plus fuel, repairs and maintenance required.

Buying a car is crazy expensive here. I often send ads for used car sales to a friend in the US for the shock value. Comparing the most popular cars here, Toyotas are almost always the most expensive used vehicles. A 30-year-old Toyota SUV can cost you $15,000-$20,000.

I'm joking but... sometimes I think that used cars seem to *increase in value here*, after they leave the lot.

Gas and diesel hover around $5-6/gallon. It has always been that price, long before the prices went up in the US.

Utilities: Electricity, water, and internet are generally affordable in Costa Rica, although prices may vary depending on usage and location. Monthly utility bills for a small condo or house could range from $80 to $300 (*más o menos*), depending on factors such as energy usage, water consumption, and internet service provider.

Entertainment and Activities: If you live near a city, you'll have access to cultural events, movie theatres and other experiences that are usually hard to find at the beach and in rural parts of the country. There are a few movie theatres outside of the metropolitan areas, but they are few and far between. Fun fact: the only movie I've seen in a theatre since moving here was Top Gun. *Because, well, how could I not?*

Beaches are *usually* free unless they're in a National Park or on private land. Once you move here and are no longer on a tight travel schedule, you'll have more time to explore and rather than paying the exorbitant tourist fees, you'll be able to find some of the lower cost and free activities in the area where you're living.

6

Location Location Location

Finding a location to live can be a challenging task. It's a little but "big" country, after all!

I see people ask in groups, *"Where should I live"* and of course, there's a hundred different answers. I've seen responses to just one post that included: Ojochal, Turriabla, La Fortuna, Tamarindo, Mal Pais, Atenas, Puerto Viejo... get where I'm going here? Each of these towns is drastically different from one another!

Everyone has a different opinion, and everyone's needs, wants and likes are different. Without personally knowing the person who is asking, answers provided to this type of question are generally not helpful.

Personally, I've bounced around Costa Rica, living in several different regions and 17 (*yes, 17*) rentals. Just call me Goldilocks.

Whenever I work with clients, *"Where do I want to live"* is always the biggest question. A lot of people

Location Location Location

think they want a particular area... until we start talking about the pros and cons and they realize there's more to consider than just the type of location and the weather! I encourage you to do extensive research when choosing a town to call home in Costa Rica. Here are some of the factors to consider:

- Lifestyle Needs
- Cost of Living
- Commute and Transportation
- Outdoor Activities and Recreation
- Community and social interactions
- Healthcare
- Education
- Climate
- Quiet, secluded life? Busy environment with modern amenities?
- Long-term plans and goals
- Essential amenities and services
- Safety and security concerns
- Business opportunities

> PRO TIP: If you're older or have health issues, one major consideration should be medical care - is quality care easily accessible? If you have children, does the town offer enough activities for a well-rounded childhood experience?

Provincias

Alright, let's start by understanding the big picture and then we can zoom in on more specific details.

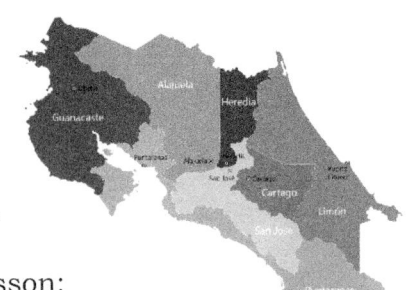

First, a geography lesson:

Costa Rica is divided into seven provinces (*states*). We have the Pacific Ocean on the west coast, Caribbean on the east coast, Nicaragua to the North, and Panama to the Southeast.

I specify Panama is to the *Southeast*, because if you hop across the border, you'll change time zones and be one hour ahead.

San José: San José is the capital city of Costa Rica and the name of the province surrounding it. We'll talk more about this region in the next section.

Alajuela: Alajuela, the city, is known as the "City of Mangoes" and is the second most populated province in Costa Rica. It is the location of Juan Santamaría International Airport, the country's largest airport. *Do take note: SJO airport is NOT in the city (or province) of San José!*

Location Location Location

Cartago: Cartago was originally the capital of Costa Rica until 1823. The province is home to the Basílica de Nuestra Señora de los Ángeles, a major pilgrimage site (*see the chapter on Holidays to learn more*).

Heredia: Heredia is known as the "City of Flowers" and the province is famous for its coffee plantations and amazing landscapes.

Guanacaste: Guanacaste has both the tropical dry forest in the Northwest as well as the rainforest-like conditions around the western half of Lake Arenal (*the eastern half, after you cross a particular bridge on the way to La Fortuna, is actually a part of Alajuela*).

Puntarenas: Puntarenas province is famous for its stunning Pacific coastline and abundant wildlife. Contrary to popular belief, it is indeed possible to find affordable living along the coast, if you choose a less touristy-type town.

Limón: Located on the Caribbean coast of Costa Rica and known for its laidback lifestyle, Afro-Caribbean culture, and untouched nature. The Caribbean side is much more remote than most other areas around the country.

A LITTLE HISTORY

Lake Arenal, located in the northern region of Costa Rica, is a part of both Guanacaste and Alajuela provinces and has an interesting story.

It's a human-made lake that was created in 1973 with the construction of the Arenal Hydroelectric Dam. Before the dam's construction, the area was a valley with small communities, farms, and forests.

The dam is one of the country's most significant sources of renewable energy in the country. A friend and I drove all around the lake trying to find the dam but couldn't figure it out. There was nothing that looked like what I'm used to seeing in terms of dams, like the Hoover dam.

To make the dam, several towns and agricultural lands were flooded, and the residents of those towns needed to be relocated. One of the original towns was "Arenal," hence why the new town to the north of the lake was named, "Nuevo Arenal" (*New Arenal*). I've never personally seen it, but apparently, if the water level gets really low, you can actually see the church steeple peeking out of the lake.

Location Location Location

Now let's zoom in on some of the popular and common towns that expats reside in. I won't be listing every possible town so remember that there are so many other options and it's important to explore and see what feels best for you and your needs and wants!

Question to ask yourself as you begin to explore: *Who are you and what type of people do you want to surround yourself with?* Different towns and communities will have different vibes.

If you need help, reach out. We can do a deep dive into location options, given your personal needs and wants. That's what I'm here for!

Beach: With almost 800 miles of coastline to choose from, there's a beach destination to suit every preference.

Considerations: The beaches are beautiful but is there enough to keep you entertained (*especially if you have children*)? Are the services you need adequate like schools, medical, and grocery stores? Can you handle the heat? Are you prepared to live with higher expenses, especially if you need to use A/C?

The temps at the coast usually range from 25°C to 35°C (77°F to 95°F) year-round. *In 2024, due to drought conditions, those temperatures increased several degrees.*

In the Pacific Northwest, popular beach towns include: Playas del Coco, Hermosa, Flamingo, Potrero, Matapalo, Playa Grande, Tamarindo, Nosara, Samara, Carillo, Santa Teresa*, Montezuma*. Rainy season: Normally May to November, with heavy rainfall in September and October. Summers are very hot and dry.

Central and Southern Pacific Coast towns include: Herradura, Jacó, Esterillos, Bejuco, Parrita, Quepos, Matapolo, Dominical, Uvita, Ojochal, Osa Peninsula*. Rainy season: Usually begins in April and extends through December, sometimes even into January in some locations. Heavy rainfall in September and October.

Southern Caribbean: Cahuita, Puerto Viejo, Manzanillo. Rainy season: The Caribbean* has a slightly different weather pattern. In contrast to the Pacific side, September and October are usually a mini summer with drier conditions.

***Special consideration:** The Caribbean, as well as a few areas along the Pacific, are remote in comparison to other places I've mentioned here. If you need medical care, shopping or services, these areas may not be your ideal location.

City: Areas around San José, Cartago, Liberia, Perez Zeldon

Considerations: San José is the most densely populated region of Costa Rica. It's the heart of the country, home to museums, theaters, hospitals, and shopping, as well as large markets and modern amenities. Question to ask yourself: *Can you handle the traffic, and all the people?* Not everyone likes city life!

WHAT'S THE GAM?

In Costa Rica, "GAM" stands for "Gran Área Metropolitana," (Greater Metropolitan Area). The GAM refers to the urban cities and towns in and around the capital city of San José.

If you want easy access to modern conveniences, like shopping malls, restaurants, and cultural events, then the city may be where you want to live. It is, however, in the middle of the country and therefore, nowhere near the beach. But an hour or so west or a few hours east and you'll be soaking up the sunshine on a sandy shore.

Climate: Mild, average temperatures range from 15°C to 30°C (59°F to 86°F), with cooler temperatures at higher elevations. The dry season *typically* spans from December to April, while the rainy season lasts from May to November.

Areas to explore around the San José region that offer a more relaxed pace of life while still providing easy access to urban amenities include: Escazú, Santa Ana, Heredia and Alajuela, Ciudad Colón.

Larger cities in other parts of the country include Liberia and Pérez Zeledón. Liberia is in Guanacaste and is very hot and dry. It has an international airport and easy access to the beaches. Pérez Zeledón, to the south, is up in the mountains, not too far from Southern beaches and temperatures are more moderate.

Countryside:

Want to be near the city but outside of all the traffic congestion and chaos?

Atenas and Grecia are two of the most popular areas for expats near San José. Atenas is known for having the best climate in the world... *of course, that's subjective*! Note: because of the proximity to Poás Volcano, when it's active some people have said there is an overwhelming smell of sulfur, plus the possibility of falling ash.

Further away from the cities, towns around Lake Arenal (which can be *very* windy!), as well as the region around Turrialba or on the outskirts of Pérez Zeledón all provide you with mild to moderate temperatures and a relaxed sense of living. La Fortuna is another option, but it can be much hotter there. Some of these areas will also get weather patterns from both the Pacific and the Caribbean so be aware that it may rain more, throughout the year, compared to other areas.

Considerations: If you're considering rural living, remember to think about accessibility to amenities, healthcare services, and proximity to larger cities for occasional outings, shopping or medical emergencies.

Mountain Regions:

Looking to slow way down? Towns like Monteverde, San Gerardo de Dota and the Chirripó region have a much slower pace of life and much cooler temperatures.

Considerations: Keep in mind factors such as access to essential services, shopping options and road conditions.

Fun fact: Costa Rica's Blue Zone

Nicoya is famous for being one of the world's five Blue Zones, regions where people live longer, compared to the global average. It has a high concentration of centenarians (*people who live to be 100 years or older*) and a culture that promotes longevity through factors such as diet, lifestyle, and social connections.

7

A Place to Call Home

Before we jump into whether you should buy or rent, let me share with you a few more factors to consider as you begin your move and think about where you want to live.

To ship or not to ship

One of the first steps to moving abroad will be dealing with your current home environment, which next to choosing a location, can be one of the hardest things to do.

I get it, deciding what to take with you, what to sell, what to donate or give away... that can be brutal if you've had a few decades of accumulating your treasures and keepsakes.

Some people decide to pack it ALL up, put it in a shipping container and move here. But there are some downsides to doing that. Here are a few reasons why...

Most homes here are sold or rented furnished so when you're deciding to ship your life here, it's something to consider whether you really need everything or can whittle it down to just the essentials.

You also might need a lot less than you think. Depending on where you live and the lifestyle you hope to have here, you might not need as much as you do in your home country.

It's costly. I knew a couple who spent $10,000 on shipping only to move into a tiny home where nothing fit (*so their house was a nightmare with stuff piled everywhere*) AND they ended up moving back to their home country in less than a year.

Risk of loss or theft. While we always hope all will go well with moving furniture and boxes, even on a short distance move, things can get broken or lost.

From local artisans to international retailers, you may be able to find everything you need to furnish your new home here. Depending on your preferences and budget, purchasing items locally may be more practical and cost-effective than shipping them from abroad.

And then there's the environmental considerations, which is a bit of a catch-22.

Shipping your household belongings to Costa Rica may help the planet by reducing the demand for new goods and minimizing waste. Reusing existing items rather than purchasing new ones can help conserve resources and lower your ecological footprint.

However, shipping in container ships contributes to environmental damage with air pollution, greenhouse gas emissions, and noise pollution, amongst other problems associated with the shipping industry.

Also, not everything you take with you may do well here. I knew someone that took all her expensive leather goods – Prada, Gucci, Dolce & Gabbana purses, clothes... only to have it all be destroyed by mold. Others have taken musical instruments and had them damaged by the humidity.

Certain things just don't do well here! Or they require a lot more maintenance and upkeep than what you might be used to.

Here's why you may want to ship your household here: There's no place like home.

Shipping your belongings to Costa Rica allows you to personalize your new space and create a home that feels like *you*. Having your belongings, whether it's cherished family heirlooms or everyday essentials, can help you settle into your new environment.

To this day, I wish I had found a way to ship my great-aunt's coffee table. It wasn't a grand piece of furniture, but it was something special that I appreciated having in my life. However, my Spanish teacher's wife, who was from México, said she would take it and that made me feel better about the situation, as I knew she would regard it as a family treasure.

Arriving in Costa Rica with your household already in place (*or, at least, on its way*) can streamline the moving process and save you time and effort.

Instead of having to seek out unfamiliar stores in unfamiliar cities and dealing with the logistics of purchasing new items and having them delivered, you can focus on settling into your new surroundings and adjusting to life in Costa Rica.

If you decide to ship, ask for quotes and references from several companies. Ask them how they'll handle losses, if they'll manage all the government fees and process all the paperwork. Also make sure you understand when to expect the items here at the port in Costa Rica and how delivery will be managed. Get it all in writing. Communication is key!

The Comfort of Expat Communities

Oh, those pesky Facebook group commentators, where keyboard warriors like to shame people for wanting to live in a city with other expats.

There really is nothing wrong with wanting to live in an "expat" community. Sure, my hope would be that you'd want to assimilate into Costa Rica culture, but just because you choose a town with expats doesn't necessarily mean you aren't finding other ways to participate and integrate.

And let me just add here, while I'm sure there are some, I don't know of many cities and communities that are exclusive to just expats. There are a lot of locals who can afford to buy homes in these communities and who also want to live in the *same type of environment* as expats that include security and other amenities.

Let's also remember that places like the US are full of expat communities. Little Italy, Chinatown, Koreatown... sometimes it's nice to be around people who understand you and where you're from, especially when you're in a new country, new culture and possibly a new language. The familiarity of home can be comforting and help you ease into your new surroundings.

And on that note, same goes for the people who say: *I would never live in a gated or guarded community.* Just because someone chooses a secure community to live in, doesn't mean they're living in a bubble.

I've been robbed and my home has been burglarized six times since moving here in 2012 (*I seem to have a dark cloud that follows me around*).

As a single female, my comfort level is to be in a place that is secure. That could mean bars on the windows and doors, a gated driveway and fenced property, or a guarded and gated community. Or some combination of all the above.

I've known <u>local</u> people that own single family homes and who have hired a guard at night to stand outside their home, while they were sleeping inside! Everyone has their reasons. *So, let's minimize the judgment, shall we?*

You may also want to ask yourself: *Is there a reason why they have so much security? Is there something I don't know?*

And on that note...

Safety First

I share more about this in the Dark Side of Paradise chapter, but some people don't like talking about safety concerns because it threatens not only the bubble they're living in, but also their investments if they happen to own a home or business here.

Crime does happen here and it's no longer just "petty theft." In just the last few years, I have personally known people who have lived here for decades, whose homes were broken into and who were nearly beaten to death.

So, before choosing a location, research the safety situation in the area you'll be living in. Understand the local laws, crime rates, and any areas to avoid. Check out the OIJ "CR Safe" app (*but remember only crimes that are reported will be available in the stats and most go unreported*).

Join Facebook groups for the town where you'll be living and use the search bar to look for keywords like: robbery, thief, theft, burglary, crime, etc...

Look for groups specifically for crime in Costa Rica, especially those in the area you're thinking of moving to. Ask local friends if there are any "secret" security groups. Sometimes these groups are created to ensure that only local people, *and not tourists*, can find them and join.

Stay updated on current events and any safety advisories for both your local area and the country. Read local newspapers or online news sources to stay up to date.

Make sure your home is secure. Use sturdy locks on doors and windows, and consider installing a security system, as well as bars, gates, walls and razor wire, if necessary.

Avoid displaying expensive items such as jewelry, electronics, or large amounts of cash in public or when people are working at your home. Keep valuables secured when not in use. (*but be aware that safes can be broken into and even pulled out of concrete walls*).

Be aware of your surroundings when out in public places. Avoid walking alone at night, especially in poorly lit or unfamiliar areas. Use reputable transportation services, especially at night. Avoid getting into unmarked taxis or accepting rides from strangers.

Keep your passport and other important documents in a secure location. Make copies and store them separately in case of loss or theft. Some banks around the country offer safety deposit boxes.

If something feels unsafe or uncomfortable, trust your instincts and remove yourself from the situation.

Be aware of cultural norms and customs that may have an impact on your safety. For example, while I wouldn't say this applies to every Tica, several have told me that they wouldn't go out at night by themselves. This is what they were taught and is a cultural norm for them.

Of course, for someone like me, that seems odd. This isn't just about local women going out at night socially, but even to the grocery store. They were taught not to do so by themselves.

Have the numbers for police, fire and hospital in a visible location like on your fridge.

Real talk... the few times I needed emergency services, I haven't had much luck when I called 911 but when I called direct to the local station, I've had more success. I've also heard (in 2024) that a 911 app is coming soon and hopefully that will provide better service and emergency care.

8

Buying vs Renting

The question of whether to jump right into buying property or take a more cautious approach by renting first can spark, once again, spirited debates among expats. But fear not, whether you're a spontaneous shopper or a detailed planner, there's a property – whether rented or purchased – waiting just for you in Costa Rica.

Real talk... For many years I subscribed to the idea that you MUST rent before buying a home or lot. However, as the years have passed and in my work as a relocation counselor, I've found that for some people, buying before moving or upon arrival really does work better for them.

If you're unsure about whether to rent or buy, read on...

Are You Spontaneous or Cautious?

Renting before buying can be advantageous for some but it may not always be feasible or desirable for everyone. In the end, the decision to rent or buy will depend on individual circumstances and long-term goals.

Here's a *snapshot* of things to consider, to help you decide what is best for YOU.

Purchasing a home requires a significant amount of money. However, owning a property can be a long-term investment, providing potential appreciation in value and stability in housing costs.

On the other hand, renting offers expats more flexibility and fewer financial obligations upon arrival. Renting eliminates the need for "cash on hand" and allows expats to avoid the risks of being a homeowner, like the possibility of property depreciation and maintenance expenses. However, renting may lead to fluctuating rental prices, limited control over the property, and the possibility of frequent relocations.

I was talking with a Tica friend who told me she bought land recently because the owner of where she was living sold the place and she had to find a new rental. The rentals she was looking at were "shacks" (*as she put it*) for $800 or more!

Owning a home provides a sense of stability in a foreign country. It can provide a sense of permanence, belonging and security, helping you integrate into the community.

Conversely, renting *may* result in a more transient lifestyle. That said, renting offers the flexibility to explore different neighborhoods and cities without the commitment of being locked into one location.

Owning a home means you'll have to manage property upkeep, repairs, and renovations, which can be particularly challenging in a foreign country with different building standards and regulations. *Especially if you buy an older home and are unsure exactly how it was built.*

Always keep this in mind:
Things are different here.

Homeowners also have the financial burden of both anticipated and unexpected expenses, such as property taxes or repairs, which may strain your budget and add complexity to your life here on the Rich Coast.

In contrast, renting *usually* alleviates expats from many maintenance responsibilities. Property owners are typically responsible for maintenance and repairs, allowing renters to have a home base without the added stress homeownership can bring.

However, renters may encounter limitations on what they can and cannot do, depending on their lease agreement and the mood of the owner or property manager, which can impact their ability to create a comfortable living environment.

> Whether you buy or rent, something to be aware of: make sure you understand that the "size" given in an advertisement might include both the interior and the exterior under the roofline (patios, sidewalks, outdoor sink areas, etc).

A few more reasons to consider renting first:

Renting allows you to get a better understanding of the local real estate market, including prices, neighborhoods, amenities, and potential challenges. This firsthand experience can help you make a more informed decision when it comes to buying property.

Living in a new country can be a significant adjustment, and renting allows you to acclimate to the local culture, lifestyle, and community before committing to a long-term investment.

For expats who are uncertain about their long-term plans in Costa Rica or who may not have the financial resources to purchase property immediately, renting is often the better option.

HOA vs Non-HOA

In another life, many *many* moons ago, I worked as a community manager for Homeowners' Associations. I was actually really good at my job, but I despised it. And I swore I'd never live in an HOA in Costa Rica. *But never say never, right?*

Whether you rent or buy, you may end up living in an HOA. HOA's can be found in both condo developments as well as single-family home communities.

There are some pros to living in an HOA (*and there are some cons*). And know that it's VERY dependent on the community. Some HOA's might be super lax while others might be over the top micro-managing regimes. Some might be well organized and maintained while others don't know what they're doing, there is no budget, and everything is falling apart.

With an HOA, you might get increased property values, security, and amenities like a pool or other common areas as well as road maintenance.

The downside is that you have to obey the rules and possibly, depending on the Board, someone is always watching. Monthly fees can range from below $100 to several hundred. Regulations on pets, architectural changes and other rules can be either seen as a positive or a negative, depending on who you ask and what's being restricted.

Not living in an HOA, you'll still have to abide by city regulations. There are also less fees, although you'll still have to pay property taxes and any other administrative fees, if, for example, you have your home in a corporation.

However, you'll have to implement your own security measures, install a pool and other amenities and your property value may not be as protected as you'd like. You never know who is going to move in next door and build a purple house just a few feet from your property line, or worse, literally attached to the wall of your home.

You also have to deal with the city to handle any issues, which can be challenging, versus talking about your concerns with a smaller group of people in an HOA.

9

Buying

If you've decided to buy...

Whenever you decide to buy, please do extensive research and due diligence. Make sure you hire an attorney that knows what they're doing. Walk around the community, talk to the neighbors, join local Facebook groups for the area and take a look at the types of posts that are being shared.

> PRO TIP: Many people move here thinking they want to slow way down. They choose a tiny town to live in and then realize maybe they need more entertainment and services than what they can find nearby. Make sure you understand what is available in the area and think about what your day-to-day life will be like, *before you buy.*

FAQ: *Can I buy a property there and own the land?* Yes, as long as it's fully titled with no concessions.

FAQ: *Do I get residency if I own property?* That depends. (1) Your investment must be over $150,000 and (2) you still have to apply for residency and be approved.

Buying before you move

Buying property without living here full-time can, once again, have both advantages and disadvantages. Here's a quick *snapshot.*

Pros:

- Investment Potential
- Rental income
- Vacation home for when you want to get away
- Investment diversification

Cons:

- Maintenance and Management
- Legal and Administrative Issues
- Remote Ownership Risk

Is the rumor about squatters for real?

Squatters can happen in Costa Rica, but it seems it's becoming less of an issue in recent years. If your property is left unattended for long periods, especially in rural or less populated areas, it may be at a higher risk for squatters.

Hiring a reputable property management company or caretaker to look after your property while you're away can help reduce the risk of squatting by ensuring that the property is regularly checked and maintained.

If you get squatters on your land, it's important to understand the legal process for removing them and to work with legal professionals who are familiar with the process.

When Your Dream Home Isn't the Right Fit

This has happened to people I know and unfortunately, (*oftentimes*) it's harder to sell than it is to buy. Some people have taken huge losses, been frustrated with the situation, and even moved back to their home country.

That's unfortunate.

So, what happens when that dream home turns out not to be the perfect fit you envisioned? Well, you have two choices.

I knew someone who built a McMansion in one of the rainiest parts of the country. Then got angry when he realized how much it rained and essentially threw in the towel and returned to his home country.

Others have accepted that they made a mistake but realized they could stay in Costa Rica and explore different options where they'd be happier.

Just because a particular location or environment doesn't align with your expectations doesn't mean it's the end of the road for you in Costa Rica. Instead, it's an invitation to explore new possibilities and discover what truly resonates with your wants and needs.

First, rather than focusing on feelings of disappointment or regret, instead look towards the opportunities that lie ahead.

Then, take time to reflect on what exactly it is that didn't resonate with your current location. Was it the climate, the community, or the services available? Refer to the list I previously shared regarding the questions I pose to my clients about choosing a location.

Answering these questions will provide you with insights on what you're looking for in your next home and location.

Perhaps you were at the beach, the heat was too extreme, and you long for someplace cooler. Maybe the community lacked what you were looking for in terms of the types of people you wanted to call your neighbors. Or it could be that the amenities and infrastructure fell short of your expectations, leading you to explore areas with better access to healthcare, education, and entertainment options.

Once you've sold your property, I highly recommend renting this next time around, *until you're absolutely sure about the location you've chosen.* Because even if you decide "near the beach" is where you want to be, you still have almost 800 miles of coastline to figure out where you'll be happiest. That can feel overwhelming so take it slow and do your research.

Always remember to keep an open mind and remain flexible in your expectations. *Sometimes, the perfect home may be found in unexpected places.*

Each proactive step forward you take, the closer you'll be to where you truly belong.

10

Building

Living in seventeen rentals has taught me a lot about building a home in a tropical environment. I've also done extensive research into building a home and the mistakes people make.

Here's a *snapshot* of what I've learned along the way...

Hire a reputable contractor and architect. Get references from each. Overdo it on the due diligence because unless you have unlimited funds, you only get ONE shot at getting this right!

Have contractors and architects visit the site you plan to buy and give you their opinion... *before you buy.* This may be at an additional cost but it's worth it.

Before buying, ensure you have a water letter, electricity letter and that the land is properly titled without any concessions. Also ensure those letters and title are indeed for the piece of property you're buying.

Have a detailed contract with all service providers, outlining *very* specifically what is included and not included, including timelines and costs.

Confirm in the contract that the contractor has insurance for all workers, or if you need to buy it separately.

Ensure there is a warranty given by the contractor and that it is stated in the contract.

Whenever possible, hire a contractor and architect who are in your area. It will make warranty items much easier to manage.

Be aware of ALL costs. It's a good idea to add an additional 20% over the proposed amount for incidentals and unknowns. Try to have fewer of both by knowing as much about the project as possible before the construction contract is written, and the plans are developed.

You'll need to get approval not just from the City where your home is located, but also CFIA (*Colegio Federado de Ingenieros y de Arquitectos*).

Building in the dry season will usually be easier and faster than building in the rainy season.

Do not start building until you receive final sign off and permits from the city.

Be on-site AS MUCH AS POSSIBLE. If you can't be on-site, hire a third party who is knowledgeable in construction – *and who you trust* – to oversee the build.

I lived on a property where they were building another home. A local family owned the property. The owner, who lived off-site, brought a folding chair and a book every day to the site during the build to oversee the workers.

Make sure your contractor installs ventilation in the bathrooms and "p traps" (*you'd be surprised at how many houses don't have either*). If you want to flush toilet paper, you'll need to install the right size pipes to the septic tank. Make sure your contractor understands this.

I can't stress this one enough: Install weatherstripping. The last thing you want is a fer-de-lance snake coming inside your home. It's not a guarantee but if done correctly, weatherstripping will help keep out a lot of your outdoor neighbors who may want to become your roommate.

Use good quality wood throughout your home. One newcomer told me that in less than six months of finishing their build, they had to fumigate for termites and was told fumigation would have to take place every six months. That is **NOT** normal.

Building

One house I lived in extended the tile floor into the baseboards, instead of using wood. I have had so many ant nests in baseboards over the years and they are impossible to deal with! Tile baseboards were an innovative solution. The rental also had metal doors, instead of wood.

Mold AND insect mitigation. If you haven't spent much time here, you may not have noticed that a lot of local homes don't have cabinets, drawers, or closets. Part of the reason for that may be due to budgetary concerns. But also, another big reason, is because in certain areas around the country, mold likes to grow in those dark spaces and insects like to hang out and breed.

Good quality wood can help with mold and insect mitigation along with having open spaces rather than having everything closed off.

Not to say it's not possible, of course lots of homes do have closets and cabinets. But you may need to take steps to ward off invasion from both insects and mold.

Talk with your architect and builder about installing a dry room with a dehumidifier where the hose drains outside of the house. You may need to run that 24/7 so remember to include that cost in your budget for electricity.

As much as possible, think outside the box about how to mitigate the challenges of living in the tropics. Talk with your contractor to see what best practices they can recommend.

Install a whole house surge protector. While I can't guarantee that it'll protect your home from power surges, it's an added level of defense against frying your electronics, which unfortunately, has happened to a lot of people I know... including locals.

Have a slope? Plant vetiver at the start of the rainy season to help with erosion control. Actually, plant all plants at the start of rainy season. Don't attempt it in summertime!

If you're concerned about security issues, get over the idea that bars are ugly. Eventually, you won't even notice them. But you will feel a lot safer, both when you're at home and away.

To reduce issues with leaves in your gutters at the roofline, talk with your contractor about having a screen placed over them.

Install a water tank. Doesn't have to be gigantic, but having water for times when either the city tanks are empty, the spring is dried up or there's a leak in town and the water is turned off, is advantageous.

Water filters (at the meter) and water softeners are both nice to have. While the water is safe to drink, at times there may be sediment that seeps through. The water in Costa Rica is also very hard which leaves those annoying spots on shower doors and causes buildup on showerheads and faucets.

Talk with your builder and architect about water management when it rains. Ensure there is a plan in place to avoid problems during the heavy downpours that happen all over Costa Rica. Several inches of rain in one storm means you need a solid plan for water drainage, away from your home!

As a comparison, the average *annual* rainfall in Los Angeles, California is fourteen inches. But here in Costa Rica, one storm can bring five or more inches.

Some people prefer French drains because you can't see them, but depending on where you live, that may not be advisable due to the silt and debris that could end up in them. Open culverts are an option that you can maintain easily. Talk with your contractor about what is best for your property.

And last but not least... Do as little damage to the environment as possible. Plant more trees, nurture your soil, please be a guardian of the land. There is no Planet B.

Propane vs. Electricity

As I've mentioned, I'm a California girl. Which means that for the first 37 years of my life, gas just magically appeared in my stoves, ovens and heaters of my homes. Then I moved to Costa Rica. No more magic gas. I'm not a fan of propane as it doesn't feel safe to me (*personally*) and if tanks aren't in a secure place, they can be stolen.

Let's look at the advantages and disadvantages of both to help you decide which is right for you:

Pros for Propane

- Uses include heating, cooking, water heating, and appliances such as dryers and stoves.
- Tanks can be stored on-site, so you can make that cup of coffee, even during power outages.
- You are less reliant on the grid.
- Propane is substantially less expensive than using electric.

Cons:

- Propane is flammable and can pose safety risks if not handled properly.
- While propane is cleaner burning than some other fossil fuels, it still emits carbon dioxide when burned. Having a CO_2 monitor is recommended.

- Tanks require a safe space to be stored, and propane delivery may be subject to availability and scheduling issues. Like the time I ran out of gas while trying to make breakfast... on New Years Day (*when everything was closed*).

Pros for Electricity:

- Electricity, when generated from renewable sources like Costa Rica has, can be a cleaner option compared to fossil fuels like propane.
- It's convenient. No need to store a tank or get refills.
- Electric appliances typically have fewer safety concerns compared to gas appliances.

Cons:

- Some places in Costa Rica have a lot of outages and disruptions.
- Your electric bill can vary widely depending on where you live and may be subject to increases, potentially leading to expensive utility bills.
- While electric appliances are common, some applications like high-heat cooking or heating large spaces (if you're living up in the cooler mountains) may be less efficient than propane.

Some good-to-know Spanish words:

- Casa - House
- Construcción - Construction
- Terreno - Land/Plot
- Planos – Plans (not to be confused with plano, which is the paper that shows your property lines)
- Pared - Wall
- Techo – Roof
- Culvert – Cuneta
- Piso - Floor
- Puerta - Door
- Ventana - Window
- Baño - Bathroom
- Cocina - Kitchen
- Electricidad - Electricity
- Fontanería - Plumbing
- Materiales - Materials
- Herramientas - Tools
- Contratista - Contractor
- Arquitecto - Architect
- Ingeniero - Engineer
- Inspección - Inspection
- Permisos - Permits
- Presupuesto - Budget
- Proyecto - Project
- Construir - To build
- Diseñar - To design
- Acabados - Finishes
- Pintura - Paint
- Cemento - Cement

11

Renting

By law (2024), rental agreements are for three years and if paid in US dollars, the rent cannot be increased for the duration. If paid in colones, the rent can be increased yearly.

Costa Rica is generally known as a tenant-friendly country however if something were to go awry, *like the owner doesn't give you back your deposit upon leaving,* you'd really have very little recourse. Yes, you can sue them, but there is no small claims court here and it'll probably cost you more in attorney's fees, time and energy than what you paid for the deposit.

Out of the seventeen rentals that I've lived in, I gave a deposit to fourteen of them, and out of those, only three returned my deposit. *And no, I did not trash the places.* I did often leave before the contract was up *but that's because...*

I've had to deal with property managers and owners who sexually harassed me, owners who were drug addicts and made my life so much more difficult as well as property managers who didn't want to do their job.

One expat, who lived next door to the house I was renting and was being paid as the property manager, told me I needed to go to the hardware store and find a light fixture and then call the maintenance person to have it installed. *Not a light bulb.* A light fixture.

Definitely not my job as a tenant and since I didn't have a car, I'd have to pay for a taxi to a hardware store plus waste my time wandering around the store trying to figure out what kind of light fixture should be bought. That is what she gets paid to do!

One expat owner, who I learned after moving in was an alcoholic and using cocaine, tried to tell me that I stole his washer upon moving out. Now, I did move out a few days early because I knew he was on drugs and would be very difficult to deal with. But I did not steal his washer. I bought a washer, paid to have it delivered and installed, sent him a text message that I had done so, and I did not get reimbursed.

> PRO TIP: Always keep copies of communications with the property owner or manager, as well as receipts and contracts.

One owner charged me $24 for the last month's water bill. The water meter was shared between several homes. So first, there was no way for her to determine what my share was. Second, on average, my water bill in past rentals has been around $8/month *(I'm a single person, I don't use that much water!)*.

I tried to explain to her that water was included with my rent and therefore, I already paid for my portion with the last month's rent. She refused to acknowledge the common sense that I was trying to express and deducted it from the deposit. But she was one of the three owners that returned the deposit to me, so I am just grateful for that.

Some people have been amazingly lucky with their rental choices and have loved not only their rental homes but their property managers or owners as well. *It is possible.* Like I said before, I seem to have a dark stormy cloud that follows me around.

And I only shared a few of my dreadful rental stories so hopefully that hasn't discouraged you... *ready to find a rental?*

To find a rental, you can do both online and offline searches.

There are several online platforms where you can search for rental properties in Costa Rica.

Websites like Encuentra24, Craigslist Costa Rica (*not super common but some people still use it*), and Airbnb often list rental properties. You can reach out to an Airbnb host and ask if they'd consider offering you a longer-term stay.

Some local real estate agencies offer rental assistance. They can provide you with listings that match your preferences and budget. They usually get a commission from the property owner.

Joining *local* community groups in the town where you're living (*or want to live*) is the way that I've always found rentals.

More general type of Costa Rica-focused expat groups on Facebook can be a useful way to connect with locals and expats who may have information about available rentals or can offer advice on the rental process but remember, those aren't town-specific so when asking a question, be sure to give the location of where you want to live.

I also recommend visiting the area where you want to live. You can explore the area, talk to locals, look for signs in windows and in the yard, and inquire about rental opportunities directly.

12

Mother Nature

Weather

From the coast to the cloud forest, you'll find every type of climate in Costa Rica. We've even had snow! Okay, it doesn't stick for very long but some of the higher elevations, a few times a year, do get a little snowfall.

In general, coastal areas tend to be hot year-round, while higher altitudes offer cooler temperatures.

But then there's the many microclimates.

Here are a few types and locations to give you an idea:

Lowland Tropical Rainforest: The Caribbean and Osa Peninsula.

Cloud Forest: Higher elevation towns like Monteverde and the Poás and Braulio Carrillo regions.

Tropical Dry Forest: The northwest region of Costa Rica in Guanacaste.

Highland or Mountain Climate: In regions with elevation such as the Central Valley, San José, and the Talamanca Mountains.

Coastal Microclimates: When I lived in Quepos Centro, I would contact friends working or living at the beach to ask them what the weather was like before heading out. Because so many times, it would be pouring rain where I lived but 100% blue skies and sunshine *just a few miles* up and over the hill.

Arid Zones: There will be places, especially in Northwest Guanacaste, where you'll find cactus growing. Cactus!

Living in a Humid Environment

For this born and raised California girl, moving to Costa Rica was an adjustment. But a good one in so many ways. One being: my body loves the humidity.

And while humidity often gets a bad rap, let's flip the script and explore the pros, cons and how to mitigate the challenges of living in this tropical paradise.

Pros:

Glowing skin. You can remove "moisturizer" as a line item from your budget spreadsheet. Humidity works wonders for your skin. Say goodbye to dry patches and hello to a natural glow.

I was on a flight once from San José to Quepos and a Tica, who was living abroad, started chatting with me. She mentioned how my skin glowed and that I looked like I was 28. I was, I think, 39 at the time. Humidity will keep you looking young!

Green living. Did you know that being surrounded by the color green is supposed to help reduce anxiety? Humid environments are a haven for lush vegetation. Think palm trees, vibrant flowers, and dense jungles. Nature thrives in these conditions. Plant a tree and it'll be fifteen feet tall before you know it.

Endless summer vibes. You'll have Will Smith's song, *Summertime,* playing on repeat in your head. Humid environments offer a perpetual vacation feel, where flip-flops and sundresses (*or board shorts, for the guys*) are the norm year-round. Just remember, we are super close to the equator and the sun shines strongly here. Buy sunscreen in bulk.

Cons:

Frizzy Hair. While humidity may work wonders for hair volume (*at least for me it does!*), it can wreak havoc on your hairstyle. Either accept defeat or invest in a good anti-frizz serum.

Sticky Situations. Humidity has a way of making everything feel sticky, from your skin, to your clothes, to your furniture. Drink lots of water and invest in a good dehumidifier to keep things feeling fresh around your home.

Life with bugs. Humid environments are a haven for all kinds of creepy crawlies, from mosquitoes to cockroaches and everything in between.

Mold mayhem. Where there's humidity, there's mold. From bathroom tiles to forgotten corners, mold loves to make itself at home in damp environments. Stay vigilant with regular cleaning and ventilation to keep mold at bay and maintain a healthy living space.

Sweat, sweat, and more sweat. Invest in lightweight, breathable fabrics to stay cool and comfortable. And I know I already said it, but drink LOTS of water.

Mitigating the downsides of humidity

Maintaining a comfortable indoor environment starts with effective moisture control. Investing in a high-quality dehumidifier can help to regulate humidity levels in your home, keeping them within the optimal range for comfort and health.

Regular cleaning and ventilation are also crucial for keeping humidity levels in check. If you don't have AC (*or are like me and don't like to use it*), use ceiling fans to circulate air, and consider investing in portable fans for added comfort.

> PRO TIP: If you own your home, install a ceiling fan in the bathroom. It'll reduce the sweat you'd otherwise experience while putting on makeup or doing your hair.

When it comes to clothing and linens, choosing breathable fabrics like cotton or linen can help to wick away moisture and keep you feeling cool and dry. Opt for loose-fitting clothing to allow for better airflow and minimize contact with sweaty skin, reducing the discomfort associated with humidity.

To keep pesky insects away, you'll want to combine prevention with natural repellents. Start by eliminating standing water sources around your home, as these serve as breeding grounds for mosquitoes and other pests.

We have dengue here which is often said to feel "bone crushing." *As someone who lives in pain every day, trust me, this is not something you want to experience.* Also, contrary to what some people believe, dengue can exist anywhere in the country... it's not just found in the rainforest.

Regularly empty and clean standing water from bird baths, flowerpots, and culverts to prevent water from accumulating.

Use natural insect repellents such as citronella candles, essential oils, or plant-based bug sprays to deter mosquitoes and other insects. Planting herbs and flowers like citronella, lavender, lemongrass, catnip, citronella and marigolds in your garden can also help to create a natural barrier against unwanted pests.

> PRO TIP: If you love herbs, one of the first outings for your garden should be to the Arca Verde (the Green Ark Foundation) in Heredia.
> *You can thank me later...*

Remember how I mentioned weatherstripping? Inside your home, seal any cracks or openings in doors, windows, and screens to prevent bugs from gaining entry. If you don't have them, install screens on windows and doors to allow for ventilation while keeping insects out.

Regularly clean countertops and sweep floors to remove crumbs and debris that may attract pests, and store food in airtight containers to minimize the risk of infestation.

Use cleaning products to protect surfaces from mold growth and inhibit the spread of spores. Clean and disinfect bathrooms and kitchens regularly to remove mold spores and prevent them from taking hold.

When cleaning mold-prone areas, use a mixture of water and white vinegar to kill mold spores and inhibit their growth. You can also add a few drop so of thyme essential oil but be *very* careful with that oil around pets. <u>Do not</u> let your pets near it.

Stay hydrated by drinking plenty of water throughout the day, and avoid caffeine and alcohol, which can contribute to dehydration.

Why shouldn't bleach be used for mold mitigation?

When I lived in California, bleach was a HUGE no-no. I was working as an HOA manager when "black mold" was the hot topic of discussion and learned more about mold than I ever wanted to know.

In Costa Rica, mold management can be a challenge. But the only people I know talking about "black mold" are the foreigners. Locals who I know just deal with it, without making it into a serious issue.

While bleach is often considered a common solution for mold mitigation, there are several reasons why it should not be used:

Bleach can lighten the color of mold and remove surface stains, giving the appearance that the mold is gone. However, it does not kill mold at its roots, which means it can regrow and spread if not properly addressed.

Bleach is corrosive and can damage surfaces over time. It's also a harsh chemical that can have negative effects on the environment.

How to be less harmful to our bodies and the environment? Use vinegar-based solutions or check out alternative bleach products that work well, without all the negative side effects.

Mother Nature

Drought in a rainforest? REALLY?!

As I finish writing the first edition of this book, we're wrapping up a year-long drought in the 2023/2024 season. I told a newcomer in August 2023 that we were in a drought, and she laughed at me, telling me that I must be *loca.*

Friendly reminder to new expats: *Toto, we're no longer in Kansas.* You absolutely must remove the lens' you wear from your home country.

I'll say it again... *Life is different here.*

When we talk about a drought in Costa Rica, it means a season of insufficient rainfall compared to the norm, which can have significant implications for water resources all around the country, even if there are still tropical storms happening around the country.

And it's really not a laughing matter. Many towns around the country have literally run out of water. Water sources like springs, rivers and wells have dried up. Water tanks for towns and communities are dry.

I have been in situations, in different parts of the country, where the water was turned off every single night, and sometimes even for a few hours during the day as well, in order to give the tanks time to refill. Other places have to bring in water, in tanker trucks.

How does this happen? Let me introduce you to a phenomenon that has a major impact on the weather. And how it differs, depending on where you are in the world.

La Niña and El Niño

La Niña and El Niño are a part of the El Niño-Southern Oscillation (ENSO).

La Niña

In Costa Rica, this phenomenon often means gearing up for a rainy season like no other. The country receives above-average rainfall, which may sound refreshing after a hot summer, until you realize it can lead to some serious issues. Flooding and landslides become a concern, especially in regions with steep terrain.

Now, flip the coin and head over to California. Here, La Niña paints a different picture. Instead of rain, it brings drought. The air gets drier, the ground is desperate for water, and the risk of wildfires increases dramatically.

El Niño

El Niño brings warmer water to the Pacific. In Costa Rica, this often translates to a drier outlook. There's a lot less rainfall, leaving behind dry fields and water shortages in towns around the country. It means a VERY hot summer and warmer than normal temperatures during winter.

But hop over to California, and El Niño brings a lot more rainfall, providing much-needed relief from drought. Suddenly, reservoirs fill up, hillsides turn green again, and there's hope for the thirsty land. However, it's not all sunshine and rainbows. Heavy rainfall can lead to flooding and mudslides, creating a new set of challenges for Californians.

Volcanoes, earthquakes, fires, floods...

Have you heard of the Ring of Fire (*and no, I don't mean the song*)? It's a horseshoe-shaped area in the Pacific Ocean, with intense seismic activity and frequent volcanic eruptions. And guess what? Costa Rica is a part of that.

We have nearly daily earthquakes here, but most are so small that you never feel them. The biggest one that I have experienced was the September 2012 earthquake off the Pacific Coast. It was 7.6

which is HUGE. Fortunately, little damage was done, all things considered.

I had just moved into a new place, and it was an interesting way to get to know my new neighbors. Especially when we all hopped into the back of a truck and headed to higher ground due to the tsunami alerts.

Pre-move, I was traveling here during the January 2009 earthquake that took place near Poás. A few days after, I happened to be staying near there and took a drive through the region. It was disheartening to see how much damage it caused to the region, and to the homes of people living there. Many residents were displaced.

Fires are common in the dry season, especially around the Nicoya Peninsula. Fires lead to scorched earth which can cause landslides, flooding and other issues during the next rainy season.

Floods and landslides are common throughout the rainy season. If you know a tropical storm is coming, it's best to be prepared with food, water and charged devices. Stay at home until it passes. Being out on the road can be dangerous and being stuck in a flood is not only dangerous for yourself but will likely damage your car beyond repair.

Some towns, like Quepos, Paquita and Parrita, flood frequently. Quepos was built below sea level and Parrita and Paquita are both next to rivers that overflow. Other towns around the country, even Tamarindo and Nosara, which are in the dry Northwest, can also flood.

We have a few volcanoes that are minimally active right now, including Rincón de la Vieja, Poás and Turrialba. These parks are usually open but due to volcanic activity, they can be closed without notice. Usually, it's smoke and some ash that comes out, but generally no lava.

Arenal, the most famous volcano in Costa Rica, has been inactive since 2010. It is *not* dormant but rather simply in a resting state.

And the good news is that *usually* Costa Rica isn't in the natural path of hurricane formation on either coast. We have a lot of severe tropical storms but the most I've ever seen here was a Category 1 hurricane. Of course, with climate change, we are seeing weirder weather and so it's difficult to predict what will happen.

Winter and Summer

Yes, Costa Rica is above the equator but since we're just 8-10 degrees away, our seasons are reversed from the Northern Hemisphere. *Most* of the country will experience summertime and dry conditions from December(ish)-April(ish) and we'll have winter / rainy season from May(ish) – November(ish).

The Caribbean has different weather patterns however and they can experience summer-like weather in September and October.

Oftentimes the Lake Arenal area (and other locations in the middle of the country) can also experience varying weather patterns as they may get weather from both the Pacific and the Caribbean sides of the country.

Kids who are in the public education system and some private schools are usually out of school for "summer" from December through the first week of February, which also usually coincides with the coffee harvest.

So when is Springtime or Autumn?

Being so close to the equator, Costa Rica only has two seasons. Rainy (winter) and dry (summer). But we do have flowering trees throughout the year which are gorgeous!

13

Moving with Children

I don't have children. My body said NOPE when it came to conceiving but knowing parents with school age kids here, plus having studied psychology and child development while at University, I'll share a few tips on how to prepare and what to consider.

- ✓ Living abroad is an opportunity that can enhance your child's personal growth, cultural understanding, and overall well-being.
- ✓ It encourages children to expand their worldview (*something I am all for!*), experiencing a different culture, foods, holidays, and celebrations.
- ✓ Becoming fluent in a foreign language can provide an amazing opportunity for future careers.

Now let's explore why it might be difficult and how to manage the downsides.

- They may feel sad about packing up their life, especially if there are things they can't take with them.
- They may experience culture shock. It can feel overwhelming to adapt to a new culture and language, and they may feel anxious and homesick.
- If they have a tough time learning the language, that can lead to frustration and feelings of isolation.
- Making friends in a new culture and language can be challenging. They may feel lonely or excluded.
- Children may find it difficult to adjust to how schools are run here.
- Moving away from extended family, friends, and familiar surroundings can be emotionally challenging for children. They may miss the comfort and support of their friends.
- Moving to Costa Rica may mean developing a new cultural identity, something they may not fully understand right away.

Here are some tips on how to talk with your child about moving to Costa Rica:

- ❖ If you're nervous, they will be nervous. Be confident, positive, optimistic.
- ❖ Address their feelings and concerns. Practice patience if they seem to come

around to the idea and then get anxious again.
- ❖ Tell them about Costa Rica. Highlight all the amazing experiences you'll have as a family and all the friends they will meet along the way.
- ❖ Ask them for their opinion. Involving them allows them to feel a little more in control and grounded.
- ❖ Set them up with a way to stay connected to friends and family back in your home country.

Education

You'll want to extensively research the available schooling options. And remember again what I said earlier: *things are different here.*

Consider factors such as curriculum, language of instruction, extracurricular activities, and tuition fees.

Also remember to have copies of educational credentials or transcripts (*both for yourself and your children*). And make sure you have the vaccine records for all members of your family. If you are seeking residency, both sets of records may be a requirement.

Private schools

There are hundreds of schools all around the country and so many different types of schools. Unschooling, Montessori, Waldorf, and religious schools to name a few. You'll want to make sure the private school you choose has the proper accreditations.

> Good to know: "Colegio" in Spanish means high school... Not college.

The top private schools that I have seen with solid recommendations over the years are:

Lincoln School, Country Day School, The British School, Costa Rica International Academy, Del Mar Academy, La Paz, Educarte, Journey School, Tide, European School, American International School (AIS), Berkeley Academy

Public schools

Just like everything else, putting your child in the public school system has its pros and cons. They will often learn to speak Spanish faster, make local friends, and help them integrate and immerse into Costa Rica culture.

The downside is that the instruction received may not be what you're used to or hoping for.

Your child might be in a classroom with students much older or younger. If you're living in an area that has a small school, there could be one teacher for 20 children of all ages. Or a few teachers, teaching multiple grades simultaneously.

You need to ask yourself if your child is really getting the quality instruction that you want them to have, to prepare them for college or entering the workforce.

Odd schedules. While some schools have longer days, I also know of kids who only attend school three hours a day and even more strangely, one day it's in the morning, the next day it's in the afternoon, then the morning, and so on. If you work or have other obligations, the alternating schedule could prove difficult to manage. There are also "night schools" for teenagers.

Another consideration is that when a teacher is out, for whatever reason – *parental leave, teachers' strike, sick day, etc* – there are usually no substitute teachers. That could mean a day that your child misses... *or months.*

Bullying occurs in both public and private schools. Kids sometimes keep their troubles to themselves, particularly if they think their parents are excited about something (*like living in Costa Rica*) and they don't want to let them down. Ensure your child feels comfortable talking to you about anything that's bothering them.

Homeschooling... is it legal?

There is an ongoing debate whether it's legal. My understanding is it's legal (2024), although there are certain conditions to be met and (as a legal resident) you must register with the ministry of education. An attorney can help you navigate the process and make sure you're legally set up.

Reality vs Fantasy

I connect with a lot of expats who want their children to grow up in the small-town communities of Costa Rica. They often have an idealized notion of what that means. *Here are a few things to think about:*

Not all towns have sufficient options to keep children entertained. Some do, many don't.

Parents say they want their children to detach from their digital devices. Without realizing *lots* of local children have smart phones and gaming systems and have the same issues as kids in other countries when it comes to being glued to a screen, 24/7.

Be sure to plan for those rainy days, which can sometimes last for several days in a row. Games, movies, books... something to keep them entertained when they can't play outside.

In some towns, the way that people present themselves may be different from what you're used to or comfortable with. I'm saying that cautiously so as to not offend, but I know parents who don't want their kids to grow up around certain types of "*visuals*".

If you walk around some towns during the day, you may notice some women dressed in clothing that others would consider inappropriate. There may also be people using drugs openly in community spaces.

I've known parents who did not want their children exposed to that sort of element on a daily basis. I believe it's something you should be aware of (*and on the lookout for when choosing a location*) and then you can decide what is best for you and your family.

14

Moving with Pets

The good news is... there is no quarantine requirement in Costa Rica. But getting your furry family members here can cause a lot of pet parents stress.

The actual process is pretty straightforward, but I understand feeling anxious about traveling abroad with your cat or dog. Let's see if we can reduce some of that anxiety.

> PRO TIP: The more stressed you are, the more stressed your pet will be. As I said in the beginning of this book, the more knowledge you have, the better prepared you will be... which will (*often*) result in less stress and more ease.

Your first step is to contact the airline you're traveling with and confirm they will accept pets, and more specifically your breed of pet.

Ask them what the requirements are for either in-cabin or below as well as what are the costs so you can budget appropriately. Make sure they know what month you are traveling as there can be restrictions depending on the climate, both in your home country as well as Costa Rica.

Some pet parents have said they purchased an additional seat on a regular airline for their pet. Talk with the airline to see what the options are.

While you're on the phone with them, ask them to walk you, step by step, through all the procedures so you feel comfortable. Don't be afraid to ask questions!

Understanding what will happen when you arrive at the airport will help ease a lot of the stress you may be experiencing.

There are also private planes that are dedicated to taking you and your pets to Costa Rica. More expensive, yes, but oftentimes a lot less stress.

Once you have determined how you're getting them here, then you need to talk with your vet. Ensure they know what steps need to be taken in order to process all the paperwork correctly with the government and in the appropriate time frame.

They will also need to administer any necessary vaccines, and do an examination, within a certain number of days before your departure.

Once at the airport, if you're taking your pet in-cabin, you'll first need to get them through security. With a dog, that's relatively easy but please make sure they're on a leash. You don't want them getting scared and running off.

With a cat, security is likely going to require you to take your cat out of the carrier.

When I took Harmony through security, they wanted me to take him out in the middle of San Francisco Airport and just hold him. I said *absolutely not*. So they agreed to put us in a little makeshift room without a ceiling, I took him out of the carrier and then the carrier was put through the x-ray machine.

We had a layover in Miami, and we were flying American, so I used the Admiral's Club shower to let him out of the carrier. I had a portable litter box with me in my carry-on and put out food and water for him. He wanted nothing to do with any of it. *Pobrecito...*

Upon arrival at Liberia airport, it was a simple check of the paperwork by an agent. They didn't even look at Harmony.

The hardest part for Harmony after arrival was adjusting to the humidity. He was also California born and raised so while the heat wasn't too much of an issue, I could tell the humidity was hard on him.

Food and other necessities

Finding high quality food and accessories (*like a domed litter box*) has proven to be a challenge, even now so many years later. However, there are more and more pet stores offering better quality products and I'm hopeful that trend will continue.

Those stores tend to be more so in the city though, not so much in the rural, mountainous and coastal areas. But you can always ask your local vet if they can find and order a certain product for you.

What to be aware of

One of the worst threats to pets here, if living in a more rural, mountainous, or coastal area, is the snake population. If your dog or cat is outside, remain vigilant and take precautions such as keeping pets on leashes and avoiding areas where snakes are known to inhabit.

Besides the venomous snakes, other snakes, like the boa constrictor, will actually attempt to eat small dogs and cats.

Cane toads are abundant here, especially during the rainy season. When pets encounter the toad, even if they just simply lick or touch them, the toad releases a poison from its skin (bufotoxins) which is toxic. Symptoms include drooling, seizures, cardiac abnormalities, and even death if left untreated.

> Talk with your vet about what kind of first aid emergency supplies to have on hand.

In some areas around the country, vets will offer emergency service and at-home care. Actually, as I write this, my vet is indeed coming to my home in just a few hours to take care of one of my cats.

I recommend posting in a local Facebook group, *before arrival*, to ask for veterinary referrals in the area where you'll be living.

15

Residency

In this chapter, you will find the most frequently asked questions about residency.

Let's start off with the three most common types of residency:

Pensionado (Pensioner / Retiree): For people who receive a pension or retirement income. To qualify, you must provide proof of a monthly pension income of at least $1,000 (as of 2024) from an ongoing source, like a government or private pension fund.

Rentista (Still Working): Rentista residency is for people who can prove a steady income from a job. You must be able to prove a guaranteed monthly income of at least $2,500 for at least two years (as of 2024). Contrary to what the name suggests, it is not related to renting. You could own a home and still be a "rentista".

Inversionista (Investor) Residency: For people who invest in real estate or a business. The required investment is $150,000 (2024). In an Instagram post that I saw recently, a law firm claimed that it's still $200,000 – but the law changed in 2021. *Make sure your attorney knows what the laws are!*

All three options for "temporary residency" lead to permanent residency which, once obtained, means you are free from "restrictions." *i.e.* you can legally work, and most banks want you to have permanent residency before they give you a credit card, mortgage or car loan.

You can also obtain residency if you have a baby here in Costa Rica or if you marry a local person.

However...

1. Permanent residency is a misnomer. Once you have your DIMEX (residency card), you will still have to renew it every few years... unless you have a baby here (*which gives you residency which can lead to citizenship*) or marry a local (*which can give you citizenship after two years, versus residency*),

The number of years given for renewal seems to vary from person to person, I've seen a range of 2-5 years for renewals of permanent residency.

2. You are first granted temporary residency. That needs to be renewed in two years and then after another two years, you can request permanent residency. Most people start the "change of category" process around the three-year mark.

Documents you will need for the initial application process include:

- Birth certificate
- Marriage certificate, if applicable
- Criminal background check
- Proof of income
- Valid passport
- Passport photos
- Fingerprints
- You may also need your vaccine card (*yes, from childhood!*).

This list is not exhaustive but rather a reminder of the things you need to bring with you when you move, or to obtain upon arrival.

You'll need to get certain documents like your birth certificate translated and "apostilled." There are also deadlines that must be met as the documents are only valid for a short period of time. You may also need school diplomas.

While it can be done on your own, I recommend seeking out the assistance of an immigration attorney.

How long does residency take to get approved?

This is one of those questions that has no good answer. There is no rhyme or reason why some people get an almost immediate response within a few months and others wait for years. And it is generally not related to the attorney handling the matter. I'm sending you good vibes that your application will be processed quickly!

Just as I hit publish on this book, the law changed about residency and driving licenses. Here's the updated snapshot!

If your application for residency *has not been submitted*, you must do border runs according to the stamp in your passport. It will have a number on it that indicates the number of days you're allowed to stay in the country.

If your application for residency *has been submitted* (called "*en trámite*"), as of May 2024, you are allowed to stay in the country and continue to drive but as the law has just come out, I am still getting clarity around the regulations. My understanding is that you may need to "homologate" your license and obtain a Costa Rica license. Some articles say your home country license would still be valid, others say it is not valid. I am looking into this further and will provide updates, when I have clarity. You'll learn what homologation means in the Driving, Road Rules & Safety chapter.

How to do a border run

> PRO TIP: There is a myth that has circulated for a long time that you're required to stay out of the country for 72 hours. That is inaccurate.

A "border run" is when you leave the country to renew your "passport visa." You can go on your own or there are services offered around the country that will take you to the borders and help you with the process of going across and back. Service providers will often post in local community groups, offering the dates of when their next trip is to the border.

As of 2024, if you do a border run to Nicaragua, you can cross and return in the same day. Sometimes they may make you wait a few hours, but most people report it's an easy turn-around trip.

However, in Panama, depending on the agent you get, you might be required to stay overnight. They may also require you to show proof of money in the bank (usually $500).

For both locations, or if you travel by air, you will need to show proof that you're leaving the country again in 180 days. Even if your residency application has been submitted, that paperwork will not be accepted by the immigration agent. You **must** have an exit ticket (2024).

And remember, it's at the agent's discretion to give you however many days she or he feels like. It could be 180. It could be 10.

Keep in mind that immigration laws and procedures are subject to change, so please check what the most up-to-date requirements and regulations are, prior to doing a border run.

Perpetual Tourist vs. Proud Resident

Personally, I believe that if you're going to make Costa Rica "home," you should go through the process to become a resident. But I also understand there are many reasons why people don't, so here I'll share with you the pros and cons of both.

The Perpetual Tourist

I know, dealing with the Costa Rican government agencies can be a pain. It's a whole lot of money, paperwork, processing time and patience that is required. It's not for everyone. Being a perpetual tourist means you don't have to deal with any of that.

The downside is... As a perpetual tourist, you may experience a lack of stability. Depending on your nationality and visa status, you may encounter limitations on the duration of your stay in Costa Rica.

Constantly border-hopping can become a logistical challenge, especially if you don't live near a border. It can also be expensive, depending on how many days you receive from the immigration agent and how often you need to leave the country.

The Proud Resident

One of the biggest advantages of the resident lifestyle is the stability and security it provides. Residents have a permanent home base from which to explore Costa Rica (*and beyond*) and can enjoy the peace of mind that comes with knowing they don't have to worry about leaving.

It also means that should, *let's say*, a pandemic happens, you are legally allowed to both stay in the country and leave and return, if necessary. Perpetual tourists who left, either before the borders closed in 2020 or on one of the expatriation flights, were not allowed to return until the borders reopened.

And bonus! You can use the resident line at the airport and get discounts on national parks as well as some local airlines. Some private tourist attractions also offer resident discounts.

On the other hand... applying for residency can be a bureaucratic nightmare, involving paperwork, fees, and potentially long wait times. You'll also need to budget for attorney's fees (*if you decide not to file for residency on your own*) as well as costs to maintain your residency status.

No judgment here. The right choice depends on your individual preferences, priorities, and circumstances.

What about Law 9996?

This law is a tax incentive and was finally approved in 2023 (*it was actually approved two years prior but pending final signatures and publishing in La Gaceta*) to allow people who have been approved for residency to bring in used household goods and two vehicles tax free.

However, the fine print is a bit of a nightmare and most of the people I know who have considered it, decided against it. One of the biggest downsides is that you cannot sell the vehicle(s) for at least ten years, or you will owe the taxes on them, when sold. That can be costly. If you're unsure if you're going to make a permanent home in Costa Rica, it's a cost you'll want to factor into your budget.

I recommend speaking with an attorney to review all the regulations and restrictions and to help you decide what is best for you.

What about the Digital Nomad visa?

Costa Rica does offer the digital nomad visa but with the recent change in the law regarding how many days you can stay in the country (*from 90-180*), it isn't as necessary, especially since you can only renew the visa once, which means you'll be here for two years. Doing three border runs (*if you receive 180 days each time*), isn't as difficult compared to when it was 90 days.

It also doesn't permit you to use the time spent here towards a temporary residency application.

And of course, there are hoops you must jump through with the application process, such as providing financial documentation, proof of health insurance, etc.

Can I become a citizen?

Yes, there are a few ways to become a citizen in Costa Rica and receive a "*cédula*" (citizenship card). First, you need to ensure your home country permits dual citizenship. Marrying a local or having a baby here is the fastest and most direct path to becoming a citizen.

But if those aren't options for you...

If you've had legal residency for seven years (*five if you're from Central America or Spain*) and if you're under 65, you will need to pass a full day test that includes both Spanish comprehension and social studies, as well as sing the national anthem.

If you're over 65, you do not need to take the test (*or sing...*).

In addition to the test, there are requirements such as character references, background checks, and proof that you've been living in the country for seven years (the actual days are

Residency

counted so if you leave, those days are excluded from the total count).

For those that get citizenship, you will receive a "*cédula*", not a DIMEX card.

> "Cédula" means identity card but while some people call the DIMEX a "cédula," it's really not the same. Cédulas are for citizens and are similar to a US social security card (*but rather than keeping the number secret, everyone shares it freely here*).
>
> Here's why I don't recommend calling the DIMEX a "cédula": if you're using an online system here and need to input your identification number, there are usually at least two different categories to choose from. You'd choose either DIMEX or another option related to having an identification card as a foreigner. Choosing "cédula", in all likelihood, will return an error message that no such identification number exists, which can cause confusion and frustration.

Okay, back to getting citizenship... however, there is something else to consider. An attorney I spoke with said that while *yes*, the US permits dual citizenship with Costa Rica, Costa Rica will require you to sign a document that says you're revoking citizenship to your home country. He said, *"Don't worry, Costa Rica will never turn the paper over to the US"*, but it did give me pause. Especially since I have that dark cloud that likes to hang around.

The pause is mainly because... who knows what will change in the next 20 or so years before I'm eligible for social security or if the paper somehow does get to the US and (*heaven forbid*), I ever have to return to the US? I'm normally not paranoid but this is something significant to be aware of and contemplate *your* comfort level given all the possibilities. Please speak with an attorney if you decide to go this route.

The upside to becoming a citizen is you no longer have to deal with renewing your residency card every few years and you can vote.

The downside is this... if you're hoping it will help you be more accepted here as a foreigner, that may not be true. Some Tic@s have told me: *You will never be considered a citizen, you will always be a foreigner living in our country, a guest.*

That is a very different perspective from my own, if someone were to immigrate to the US and go through the process of becoming a citizen. But Costa Ricans have a high degree of nationalism, for better or worse, and remember also, it doesn't mean *everyone* here feels that way!

16

Healthcare

What is Caja?

"Caja" refers to the "Caja Costarricense de Seguro Social" (CCSS), which translates to the Costa Rican Social Security Fund. It's the country's public healthcare system responsible for providing medical services, social security, and other health-related benefits to citizens and legal residents.

It is funded through contributions from companies, citizens and residents.

Even with all its faults, I'll say that "Caja" is an integral part of Costa Rica's social welfare system and plays a significant role in providing accessible healthcare to its population.

What are the problems with the Caja system?

The CCSS often struggles with inadequate funding, which means service and care needs are not often met.

Patients often face long wait times to see specialists, get diagnostic tests, and have surgeries. This can lead to delays in receiving necessary treatment. Wait times can be several months or even *YEARS*.

Example: I saw a Caja doctor in early March 2024. He requested a chest x-ray be done... end of June was the first appointment available at my local hospital. A simple lab test that will take all of five minutes has an over three-month waiting period. And I don't live in a big city with hundreds of thousands of people!

Some healthcare facilities within the CCSS system lack adequate infrastructure and equipment. Every EBAIS (*local clinic*) and hospital that I have been to has had missing ceiling tiles, paint peeling off the walls and mold on the walls and ceiling.

I even asked a friend who lives in Escazu what her local EBAIS clinic is like, as Escazu is one of the wealthiest areas of the country. She said it's just like the others, run down and in disrepair.

As far as equipment is concerned, since having severe sepsis, my lungs have been problematic. The first time I mentioned it to an EBAIS doctor, I asked if she could do the spirometry test. The doctor told me that they didn't have the equipment, but she'd just write me a prescription. I didn't take the prescription.

I'm one of those people who wants to find out the root cause of my problems, rather than just putting a band-aid on it and hoping for the best.

Another time, I was using a Q-tip in my ear (*I know, I know, no bueno*), and I thought part of the cotton had gotten stuck in my ear (which actually has happened in the past when I used a generic brand here).

I first went to the EBAIS, but the doctor told me that she didn't have the scope to look inside my ear (when I say "quality care" isn't adequate, I really do mean in both the most basic and advanced ways). Anyways, I digress… so I walked down the road to a private pharmacist and asked if she had a scope, which she did and she kindly checked out my ear at no cost.

But really, how does a primary care doctor at a national public clinic not have an ear scope?

Some patients, both locals and expats, may seek private healthcare options for better quality or faster service, which can lead to inequalities among the people here.

It is also sometimes about "*who you know.*" I've heard of people skipping to the front of the line for surgeries and other specialized care because they had an inside connection (a family member or good friend helping them), which further exacerbates inequalities.

There have also been instances of corruption and mismanagement within the CCSS, which intensifies all the other problems.

What are the pros of the Caja system?

One of the most important benefits of the CCSS system is that it provides universal healthcare coverage to all citizens and legal residents of Costa Rica. That's huge for a developing country.

This ensures that everyone has access to healthcare services regardless of their income level. It also provides emergency care to non-residents as well as tourists. As a non-resident, sometimes they'll give you a bill to pay, however some people have reported never being asked to pay.

Unfortunately, non-residents who are not given a bill is one of the reasons why the system is broke and falling apart.

Healthcare

The CCSS system offers access to healthcare services, reducing disparities in health outcomes between different socio-economic groups. Patients receive care *based on medical need* rather than *ability to pay*.

> FAQ: "I pay a lot more for Caja than other people do. Can I get preferential treatment?
>
> *No. Because it's socialized medicine. So, it doesn't matter how much you pay. Whether you pay $30 or $400/month, you're going to be treated the same as everyone else. That's the way socialized medicine works. You'll be standing outside the clinic at 6am* for an appointment and waiting just as many months or years to see a specialist as the person paying $30/month.*

*You may be able to get an appointment via the EDUS app... but in larger towns where they are serving a lot of people, you may have to go direct to the clinic and stand in the line (2024).

CCSS offers primary care, preventive care, hospital services, emergency care, and specialized treatments. Patients can access various medical specialties and diagnostic procedures (*after getting approval*) through the public healthcare system.

The CCSS operates healthcare facilities (*called an EBAIS, Equipos Básicos de Atención Integral de Salud*) across the country, including clinics and hospitals in rural and underserved areas. This ensures that residents in remote regions have access to <u>basic</u> healthcare services without the need for extensive travel.

However, disparities in the quality of care can exist between different regions and facilities.

So, if you need to see a specialist or need a test like a spirometer, you'll likely have to go to a bigger city.

What does Caja cost?

As a resident, you're required to pay into the Caja system (2024). The amount you pay is dependent on your residency category and income. As mentioned previously, it can be anywhere from $30-400+ per month.

I have heard rumors that this requirement may change (*or a PPO type system might be implemented*) but for now, those are just rumors.

What are a few of the private hospitals in Costa Rica?

Some of the most well-known private hospitals in Costa Rica are:

- Hospital CIMA San José
- Hospital Clínica Bíblica (San José area)
- Hospital Metropolitano (San José area, Liberia and clinics around the country)
- Hospital San Rafael Arcángel (Liberia)

Insurance

You may also want to supplement Caja with private care. And while paying out of pocket for private care is indeed much cheaper here than comparing it to the US, it can still cost you tens of thousands of dollars, depending on what services and treatments you're receiving.

Private insurance is available but more often than not, pre-existing conditions are not covered. Even if you select a US-based insurance company like Blue Cross.

I was healthy before my surgery in 2020 and (*unfortunately*), didn't seek out private insurance as it just wasn't necessary. That was a hard lesson to learn but that means you get to learn from my mistake.

Post surgery, post sepsis, the only condition that would be covered on a private plan for me was hypothyroidism and that would have increased my premium by 10%. Everyone's circumstances will be different.

For me, pretty much nothing else would be covered as the insurance carrier would classify any other problems as a result of having sepsis. Which for those of you who aren't familiar with it, sepsis essentially tries to rapidly kill you by attacking your immune system, and your organs. It literally means "to rot or decay". So, my entire body was damaged and now, my options for coverage would be severely limited.

NB: As I had a negative experience with an insurance agent, I won't give agent referrals in this book, but I do offer options if we work together privately.

Since really nothing will be covered with private insurance, I have chosen to use Medismart instead. It's not private insurance but rather a plan that offers discounts on health services at certain clinics around the country. It has massively paid off for me. Not just in saving money but also saving my sanity in having to deal with the public health system.

They offer medical, dental, lab work and pharmacies in many clinics around the country and are associated with Hospital Metropolitano. They even offer discounts on pet health! The cost, as of early 2024, is less than $20 a month.

Be sure to check on coverage, fees, services and locations that accept it, before getting treatment!

Medications

The Caja system includes free prescription medications. However, not all medications may be available, meaning you'll have to potentially look for them at a private pharmacy and pay out of pocket.

> TRUE STORY: I once had a Caja doctor write a prescription for me for an ear infection. She also handed me a post-it note that had the name of another prescription and said: "*The Caja medication won't actually work. If you want to heal your ear infection, you need to go to a private pharmacy and ask them for this medication instead*" (the one she wrote on the post-it note).

I've heard of some people being reimbursed by Caja for prescriptions purchased at a private pharmacy, but you'll need to talk with your doctor about what the conditions are and what is required to request reimbursement.

What medications can you get without a prescription at a private pharmacy?

You may be familiar with OTC (over the counter) medications that you can get in your home country like Motrin, Tylenol, Nyquil. But did you know that in Costa Rica, most medications can be purchased at a private pharmacy without a prescription?

The two types of medications that need a prescription are antibiotics (*usually, they have started cracking down more on that*) and narcotics. Although to manage my Post Sepsis Syndrome, I've been able to buy an over-the-counter product containing codeine, which I would have thought fell into the narcotic category. Apparently, it doesn't.

To look up what medications are available and their pricing, check out Farmacia Fischel online. This is one of the private pharmacies that has locations around the GAM. You may need to first google your prescription's generic name in Spanish, in order to find what you're looking for.

I miss HIPAA

There is no HIPAA (Health Insurance Portability and Accountability Act) here. When the pandemic happened, a few friends were telling me how it was the Nicaraguans who were bringing COVID into the country. I asked them to explain how they knew that, to which they replied: *We know someone who works at the hospital, and they told us.*

Rumors and gossip abound, especially when something like the pandemic can be blamed on someone other than a local. I mention this later in the book, but xenophobia and discrimination unfortunately very much exist here.

> QUICK TIP: When you go to a public clinic, your name will be called out by the nurse, and you'll meet with her or him first. The door usually remains open and all personal information being disclosed can often be heard by those in the waiting area. You'll need to close the door yourself if you want privacy.

Another situation that would have been a huge HIPAA violation: In one EBAIS that I went to, all of the client files were in the waiting room in an open cabinet. I'd prefer magazines to flip through while I wait but alas those don't exist in the public clinics.

In May 2022, Caja was hacked. Having a system in place like HIPAA can also reduce data security concerns.

A few health care horror stories about using Caja

When we think about our health, our hope is that we'll be well taken care of. I'm not sure why people say healthcare here is "world-class" unless they're referring to private care and are forgetting to mention that important point. The only positive stories I've heard about Caja have been related to emergency care. I'm sure others exist, I just haven't heard any.

The following stories are meant to inform you about what could happen. Prepare for the worst, hope for the best.

A few years back, a woman shared with me that she had an endoscopy without sedation. She was not informed of this before the procedure. She told me that a large man stood behind her and forcibly held her down while another health care worker stuck the tube down her throat. No sedation, no numbing, *nada.*

To say I was shocked and horrified was an understatement. Not just the discomfort, pain and nausea that she must have felt but also the anxiety and stress of being held down like it was medieval times!

Another friend told me (*several years ago now, hopefully this has changed*) that he went to the Caja dentist to have deep cavities filled and no anesthesia or numbing agents were given. He was in pain for days following and no pain meds were provided, not even acetaminophen or ibuprofen. He wanted to stay at home and rest but he had bills to pay and two children to feed so he had no choice but to work with the pain.

A local friend's wife was in the hospital for weeks with a life threatening condition. The hospital didn't have the antibiotics she needed. My friend drove all around town trying to locate the necessary medications and eventually had to drive two hours north to buy them and bring them to her in the hospital.

A woman was in the public hospital for several weeks, on a cot in a *hallway*, waiting for surgery on her broken foot. WEEKS. She wasn't able to charge her phone as there was no outlet and the nurses wouldn't let her use the outlets at their desk.

Other people I know have had to wait months for a surgery. And no, you cannot leave and just wait for a phone call. That's not how it works here. You wait in the hospital.

One woman told me that she was in the public hospital and in a room with about ten other beds (which is common in the public hospitals). But the room was co-ed (which is a bit disconcerting), and the man in the bed next to her was handcuffed to it, with a police officer sitting in the corner.

Having to be in a hospital setting is already stressful enough without having to worry about why there is a handcuffed man in the bed next you.

A few new moms, who gave birth to healthy, full term babies, have told me that a few months after giving birth, the doctor gave them a prescription of iron pills to give to their babies. Without running any tests to determine if iron was indeed low. They simply said, *this is how it's always been done, your baby needs to take these supplements.* Remember to question anything that doesn't feel right, especially if the reasoning is: *"this is how it's always been done"*.

I have my own fair share of unfortunate experiences with the public health care system.

In 2022, I went to the EBAIS and was checked in first by the nurse. She asked me if I had my tetanus shot record. I didn't, but I explained that I had it done privately in 2018. She told me that if I didn't provide proof, she would force me to have the shot, even if I didn't need it. And if I didn't allow her to, I would not be allowed to use the EBAIS services. Then she took my blood pressure. That didn't go well. Then I got a lecture on high blood pressure… even though I don't actually have high blood pressure.

One time when I received my bloodwork results, it said I was a 16-year-old boy. I asked them to update the system and they refused, saying they couldn't do it.

I was having a hard time getting my records from the public hospital and an EBAIS doctor told me that I should register a complaint with the complaint department. He wrote down the phone number on a post-it for me. When I reached out and explained the problems I was having, I was told: "*You have a bad attitude*".

That's what the complaint department told me. Because I told them that I was having a hard time getting my records from the public hospital and was asking for help.

But it doesn't matter if you have a pleasant temperament and are asking for help, if you're seen as someone who is challenging the system (ie asking for your medical records), you'll be seen as difficult… especially if you're a woman (*which we'll discuss later in the book*).

When I was being "interned" at the Liberia hospital, the same doctor told me: *Do not bring your laptop, it will get stolen.* Really? In a hospital with razor wire out front and guards at each entrance, theft is still a problem.

I also couldn't get a blanket. I was given a sheet and when I told a nurse that I was really cold, she said there was nothing she could do. So I put on my sweats underneath the hospital gown and put on my jacket, which I had been using as a makeshift pillow as there were none. Then at midnight, when I was woken up to have my blood pressure taken, the nurse was angry and gave me a lecture on how I wasn't allowed to wear my regular clothes.

The beds were manual, with a crank at the end of the bed, near the floor. There also wasn't a call button, so I suppose if I had had the surgery there, if I needed a nurse post-op, I would have had to scream for help.

This took place in Liberia and I've been told that a few of the public hospitals in the San José area might have automatic beds and possibly call buttons. Pillows and blankets, maybe not.

When I was seeking help in managing the problems associated with Post Sepsis Syndrome, I went to seven doctors in my area. Some were at the public health system, others were private.

Healthcare

None of them knew what Post Sepsis Syndrome was. Some even went so far as to boldly tell me that no such condition existed. All of them essentially told me it was all in my head.

Post Sepsis Syndrome is indeed a medical condition that about 50% of survivors experience. But most doctors, worldwide, aren't familiar with it (*because up until recently, most people either didn't survive or died within a few years after having sepsis*).

The difference between my experiences here and in the US is this: the doctors in the US were willing to learn, understand and help. The doctors here did not believe it existed and when I attempted to show them on my phone, in Spanish, what it was, they refused to look at it and learn.

I very much understand and respect why some locals may believe that the Caja system is amazing. Providing health care to an entire country is a huge win for a developing country. But it is not without its problems.

> Several Caja doctors have told me, "*The system is broken*".

These stories are all distressing events that have the potential to leave someone not just with more physical problems but also emotional and traumatic memories, making them less likely to want to go to the doctor or dentist in the future.

My hope is that either you'll remain healthy and well, or you'll have better luck than I and others have experienced.

Being an advocate for yourself

Being an advocate for your own health and wellness is essential for ensuring that you receive the proper care and support you need, especially if you encounter healthcare providers who may be reluctant to help or listen to your concerns.

Here are some steps you can take to advocate for yourself: Knowledge is power. While one EBAIS doctor sarcastically asked me, "*Where did you get your medical degree?*," understanding what your symptoms are and what might be available in terms of treatment options is imperative before you walk into the doctor's office. It can also help you communicate more effectively and (*hopefully*) receive better care.

That doctor was #7 who didn't know what Post Sepsis Syndrome and probably didn't appreciate my trying to educate him, especially since he had a female trainee in the room with him. He also

Healthcare

told me he wouldn't give me a testosterone test because I'm a woman (*which reflects poor standards of education if he doesn't understand that women can be low in testosterone*).

If you don't speak Spanish well, consider having a friend come with you who does. Be as specific as possible so the doctor can better understand your needs and concerns. Sometimes the doctors will speak English, *but not always.*

Don't hesitate to ask questions and request additional information if you don't understand. Don't let them rush you because they say they only have fifteen minutes.

Be persistent. If you feel like your concerns are not being taken seriously or addressed adequately, don't be afraid to speak up and advocate for yourself. Be persistent in seeking the care and support you need, even if it means seeking help from other healthcare providers.

Keep records of your symptoms, treatments, and interactions with healthcare providers. This can help you track your progress, identify patterns in your symptoms, and provide valuable information to your doctors.

> NOTE: Doctors at the EBAIS clinics have refused to review my medical records from private doctors and hospitals. Be prepared with as much information as possible verbally if they won't read notes from outside the public system.

Alternative care

Throughout the country, you'll find different types of holistic treatments available like acupuncture, functional medicine, naturopaths, osteopaths and many other options.

There will be more availability of holistic treatments closer to San José but some of the rural and coastal areas may also have those types of providers. I have done extensive research on this for myself, mostly using local Facebook groups for where I live and google to locate those providers who were out of the area.

What can pharmacists do?

Amongst other things, pharmacists can dispense medications, offer patient counseling and administer injections (*i.e.* B12, tetanus, yellow fever, and others).

Healthcare

Common words to use that the doctor

- Doctor – Médico, Doctora / Doctor
- Nurse - Enfermera/o
- Hospital - Hospital
- Appointment - Cita
- Emergency - Emergencia
- Prescription - Receta
- Medicine - Medicamento
- Pain - Dolor
- Fever - Fiebre
- Headache - Dolor de cabeza
- Stomachache - Dolor de estómago
- Allergy - Alergia
- Cough - Tos
- Flu - Gripe
- Sore throat - Dolor de garganta
- Injury - Lesión
- Blood pressure - Presión arterial
- X-ray - Radiografía
- Surgery - Cirugía
- Vaccination - Vacunación
- Symptoms - Síntomas
- Treatment - Tratamiento
- "I'm not feeling well." - No me siento bien.
- "Where is the nearest hospital?" - ¿Dónde está el hospital más cercano?
- "I need to see a doctor." - Necesito ver a un médico.
- "Can you help me?" - ¿Puede ayudarme?

- "I have an emergency." - Tengo una emergencia.
- "I have allergies." - Tengo alergias.
- "I have a fever." - Tengo fiebre.
- "It hurts here." - Me duele aquí.
- "I need a prescription." - Necesito una receta.
- "How much does it cost?" - ¿Cuánto cuesta?

If you have allergies to medications or food, be sure you know how to say those words in Spanish. Have it written down in your phone so that you can easily access it.

Internment

In Costa Rica, "internamiento" typically refers to the process of staying in a hospital for medical treatment or observation.

As I mentioned before, it also means you are stuck there while waiting for treatment or surgery, even if there is no scheduled date.

On the other hand, in the United States, "internment" has a significantly different meaning and historical context.

It refers to the forced relocation and confinement of a group of people, often based on ethnicity, nationality, or other discriminatory factors. One example is the internment of US citizens and residents, who were Japanese, during World War II, where they were placed in camps against their will.

So, while "internamiento" in Costa Rica relates to hospitalization and medical care, "internment" in the US refers to a form of imprisonment or confinement, often under unjust or discriminatory circumstances.

Not to make light of the latter, but when I was sent to the public hospital for internment, it did indeed feel like a prison... one which I actually attempted to escape from and had nurses running after me (*but that's a story for another book*).

Here's a pic I took outside of Liberia hospital...notice the razor wire.

A look back

As we wrap up this chapter, let's take a moment to look at how far we've come.

Back in the day in rural communities, there was a lack of modern transportation and infrastructure, so many people relied on horses for daily activities, including traveling many miles to get medical help. (*Fun fact: in some small towns, you can still see people riding horses to the local bar or supermarket*)

Telecommunications were also rare. Locals and expats who were here only a short time ago – in the 1990's and early 2000's – will tell you how there were no phones in some of the rural communities and only one payphone in the town. Even in now built-up places like Quepos... it wasn't all that long ago that they had one pay phone in town and no other options for telecommunication!

Here's a story that one of my local friends told me. First, let me introduce him. He is one of 16 children. His dad passed away a few years ago at the age of 103. His mom is still alive and 101 years old!

He resided in what was known as the town of Arenal, before they flooded the valley and created the lake. One day when he was a kid (*so this was probably in the 1960's*), he fell off his horse and broke his arm. But the family didn't have a car and it being the countryside, they didn't have any modern public transportation options.

Healthcare

The town of Arenal was probably about 25 miles from the town of Cañas – where the closest medical clinic was. So he had to ride on the horse, bouncing along unpaved roads with a broken arm.

The story here gets a little fuzzy but apparently the clinic in Cañas wasn't able to help him and so he then had to travel to San José and at one point, he told me he had to board a boat to get there! I don't know what route they were taking but let's all take a moment to be thankful for the roads and infrastructure in place today.

And thankfully, health care all around the country has improved since that time. But there is still a lot of work that needs to be done to fix the broken CCSS system.

17

Banking & Money Matters

Major banks in Costa Rica include state-owned institutions such as Banco Nacional de Costa Rica (BNCR or BN) and Banco de Costa Rica (BCR), as well as private entities like BAC, Banco Promerica and Banco Popular.

The good news is... while you're waiting in line with possibly twenty other people, you can now use your phone (*there was a time when that was not allowed*).

The bad news is... lines can be long and opening a bank account can be complicated.

> PRO TIP: *In frustrating times, it'll help to remember WHY you chose to live in Costa Rica.*

Very few banks have night drops or ATM's that accept deposits, so everyone has to go inside the bank for transactions that, in other places, would normally be handled quickly and easily outside, at an ATM or online.

Regarding opening an account, it often depends on who is on the other side of the counter. Many banks will allow non-residents to open an account, however you'll have to jump through some hoops. You may need to get reference letters from local people who bank there, basically saying you're a good person and not a drug dealing money launderer.

If you have a corporation here, whether active or inactive, you can *usually* use that to open an account as well as utilities.

While banking services are well-established, it's **_super important_** to note that there isn't an equivalent of the Federal Deposit Insurance Corporation (FDIC) found in the United States. Not even with the state-owned banks.

Unlike the United States, where the FDIC insures deposits up to a certain limit per depositor per bank, Costa Rica does not offer this option. This means that depositors bear the risk of potential bank failures. I've heard of it happening, on several occasions, where people's money went missing for no apparent reason and was never found.

ATM's and wire transfers from your home country

I can only speak to US banks but as of the time of this writing (2024), the two banks I recommend are Capital One and Schwab. They don't charge fees when you use the ATM and at least with Schwab, they reimburse you the fees that the local bank may charge at the end of the month. Fidelity is another bank that has gotten good mentions from expats.

> PRO TIP: You'll likely need to provide the bank with a US address. You'll also need a US phone number. I use a free Google Voice account that *usually* works but it needs to be connected to a US cell phone. Ask a friend or family member to use their phone number, then during setup, turn off the option to call the cell. You can make and receive calls and messages on your computer and may be able to make and receive calls and messages from your phone, using the app.

For withdrawals with an international card, Banco Nacional and Banco Costa Rica usually don't charge fees at their ATM's. (2024)

To do a wire transfer, Schwab seems to have the lowest fees that I can find. Remember that you'll get a fee from the bank in your home country as well as the bank that you're transferring the money to, which can add up.

Depending on how much you transfer, you may also need to provide proof to your bank in Costa Rica, of where the funds originated. Not providing the proof, usually in a five-day time frame, means your account can be frozen and no funds can be accessed.

How does the currency exchange impact expats?

In 2022, the colon was at 690 to $1. For people from the US at least, it was a good time to be buying anything in the country. But as I write this, the colon is now below 500, something I haven't seen since I first arrived in 2012.

That's about a 30% decrease in less than two years. Over the course of a year, it can represent a significant loss of purchasing power for individuals or businesses.

While I once saw a comment from someone in a group that the impact was only "pennies" in terms of how expats would be affected, that isn't actually accurate. Especially if you're living here on a budget.

Let's compare the cost of purchasing a home priced at 50 million colones under two different scenarios: when the exchange rate is 700 colones to $1 and when it is 500 colones to $1.

Scenario 1: Exchange rate of 700 colones to $1
Cost of the home: 50,000,000 colones.
Conversion to dollars: 50,000,000 / 700 = $71,428.57

Scenario 2: Exchange rate of 500 colones to $1
Cost of the home: 50,000,000 colones.
Conversion to dollars: 50,000,000 / 500 = $100,000

So, when the exchange rate is 700 colones to $1, the cost of the home in dollars is approximately $71,428.57, but when the exchange rate is 500 colones to $1, the cost of the same home in dollars increases to $100,000.

Not everyone is going to buy a house, but everyone has to go grocery shopping so let's look at a *weekly* cost of a grocery store bill of 50,000 colones under the same scenarios:

Scenario 1: Exchange rate of 700 colones to $1
Cost of the groceries: 50,000 colones Conversion to dollars: 50,000 / 700 = $71.43

Scenario 2: Exchange rate of 500 colones to $1
Cost of the groceries: 50,000 colones Conversion to dollars: 50,000 / 500 = $100

So, when the exchange rate is 700 colones to $1, the cost of the grocery bill in dollars is approximately $71.43, but when the exchange rate is 500 colones to $1, the cost of the same grocery bill in dollars increases to $100.

Over the course of a year, that's about $1,500 extra that you will need to spend on groceries.

Cash Only

An FAQ I often hear is, *"Can I get a loan for a car or a home as a tourist or a temporary resident?"*

The quick answer is *No*.

Recently, there have been some banks and "lending" agencies that will give expats a mortgage or car loan. But be sure to read the fine print. You may not want to sign on the dotted line after doing so.

Permanent residents have more opportunities to get a loan but again, the terms and conditions are usually not favorable or what you may be used to, from your home country. *Things are different here...*

Most banks in the US will not give a loan for a foreign investment. I have heard of people taking out lines of credit and second mortgages but those come with risks and it's best to talk with your financial advisor about the possible pitfalls.

As for banking rules regarding transferring large sums of money to Costa Rica for purchases like a car or home, there are regulations and procedures in place to monitor and control the movement of funds, particularly to prevent money laundering and other illegal activities.

When you're ready to transfer those funds, know there may be a few extra hoops you have to jump through, such as providing letters from your bank, bank statements, tax returns or other documentation about the origin of the funds.

What is SINPE?

"Sistema Nacional de Pagos Electrónicos", which translates to "National Electronic Payments System" is kind of like Costa Rica's version of Zelle or Venmo. Transfers up to 100mil (colones) are *usually* free (2024).

How it works: You can use a mobile app to send money with your phone number. However, there is no recourse if you type in the wrong phone number of the recipient. You have to request the money back from the person you incorrectly sent it to, and I have heard of instances where the money was never returned.

There is some debate on whether or not you need residency to access SINPE. I have heard of some non-residents being given access. Again, it often depends on where you bank, if you have a business here as well as, again, the person on the other side of the counter.

The ripped dollar

Ripped or damaged U.S. dollars are not accepted in Costa Rica by businesses (*there may be a few exceptions, but in general, this is the rule*).

Additionally, torn or damaged US dollars may not be accepted by banks for exchange or deposit.

True story: In 2023, I went to an ATM at one of the national banks to withdraw dollars as some of my expenses have to be paid in dollars. One of the 20's that I received had a tear in it. When I went to the bank where I have an account to deposit the money, that $20 with a tear was declined by the teller.

I then returned (*on the same day*) to the original bank, went inside and attempted to explain to the woman at the reception desk that I had just been at their ATM, and one of the 20's I received had a tear and I needed to exchange it.

NOPE was essentially the answer I received. Super unhelpful, I then tapped into my local resources to figure out what my next steps would be.

I reached out to two friends. One had an account at that bank and said he could deposit the $20 bill using the night drop at the ATM and then give me a clean $20.

The other said he knew a Panamanian who was local in the area that would exchange the $20 for a clean $20 and I'd need to pay him $1 or $2 as a transaction fee. Panama also uses dollars as their currency so it's easy for him to exchange there.

I opted for the friend with the bank account, and all went well. The torn $20 was deposited and I got a clean $20 in return.

Will that $20 bill show up again in someone else's withdrawal? Probably yes, because the bank representative is likely going to put it back in the ATM machine, just as they did when I withdrew it. My hope is that it will be a tourist from the US, and they can bring it home with them and have no problem using it or exchanging it at their local bank.

Banking

Common banking phrases

- Bank - Banco
- ATM - Cajero automático
- Withdrawal - Retiro
- Deposit - Depósito
- Account - Cuenta
- Balance - Saldo
- Statement - Estado de cuenta
- Transaction - Transacción
- Currency exchange - Cambio de moneda
- Identification - Identificación
- Signature - Firma
- PIN number - Número de PIN
- Receipt - Recibo
- Transfer - Transferencia
- Credit card - Tarjeta de crédito
- Debit card - Tarjeta de débito
- Interest rate - Tasa de interés
- Loan - Préstamo
- Mortgage - Hipoteca
- Insurance - Seguro
- Branch - Sucursal
- Customer service - Servicio al cliente
- Online banking - Banca en línea
- Mobile banking - Banca móvil
- Banking hours - Horario bancario
- Necesito hacer un depósito / retiro - I need to make a deposit / withdrawal.
- Quisiera retirar [amount] colones / dólares, por favor - I would like to

withdraw [amount] colones / dollars, please.
- ¿Puedo pagar esta factura aquí? - Can I pay this bill here?
- ¿Puedo hacer una transferencia a otra cuenta? - Can I make a transfer to another account?
- ¿Puedo abrir una cuenta? - Can I open a bank account?
- Gracias por su ayuda - Thank you for your help.

18

Cultural Awareness & Adjustment

Adjusting to a new culture takes:

- ✓ Time
- ✓ Patience
- ✓ Effort
- ✓ An open mind
- ✓ Willingness to learn

Your first step: take the time to learn about the cultural norms, values, and traditions here. It's better to be prepared than to be in a situation that you don't understand and are unsure how to handle.

Approach cultural differences with an open mind and a willingness to learn. Recognize that there *usually* isn't a right or wrong way of doing things, just *different* ways of thinking.

Zoom out and look at the situation from all the many different perspectives and possibilities. You'll see an example of that when you read the "toothbrush" story later.

Pay attention to how people in Costa Rica behave in various situations and, when appropriate, adjust your own behavior accordingly. This might mean changing how you communicate, your body language, or your manners.

If something isn't clear to you, don't hesitate to ask questions. Many locals will appreciate your willingness to learn more about their culture.

Make an effort to connect with individuals in the community. Create a network of not just expats, but also locals.

Adjusting to a new culture is a gradual process. Have patience with yourself and those around you. It's unrealistic to grasp everything immediately, and minor missteps or misunderstandings are part of the learning curve.

Awareness or Adjustment?

I like to think of our world as a place where cultures connect like a colorful mosaic.

But... moving to Costa Rica, it felt more like a monoculture than a mosaic. Not only were there adjustments to be made but I also had to figure out what I needed to hold on to, to preserve my sense of self, what makes me, "me". Even many years later, my personal beliefs and values don't always align with what's considered "*normal*" here.

What happens when you encounter cultural norms that clash with your own values? What do you do? How do you handle that?

Finding the balance between cultural adaptation and holding onto one's values can sometimes feel overwhelming. You want to do "*the right thing*," to follow the cultural norms, but in every cell of your body, it just feels wrong.

So, how do you know when to blend into the cultural framework and when to stand firm in the face of cultural differences?

First, some definitions.

Cultural awareness is the recognition and understanding of different cultural beliefs, values, norms, practices, and perspectives. It involves being conscious of your cultural background and identity *while also being sensitive to and respectful of* the cultural diversity present in society.

On the other hand...

Cultural adjustment refers to the process of adapting to a new cultural environment or setting. It can encompass various aspects of life, including social interactions, communication styles, customs, traditions, and daily routines.

Someone who moves to Costa Rica may choose to be culturally aware but not always adjust to the culture on certain things for a variety of reasons, like personal values, their own cultural identity and even just taking time to adjust to life outside their comfort zone.

When you move here, there will be both cultural adaptions that you'll need to make as well as some that you should be aware of, but it doesn't necessarily mean you agree or will adjust.

Let's look at a few examples...

In Costa Rica, there's an emphasis placed on being helpful. And while that sounds nice, it can often lead to misunderstandings and frustration.

Here's why: (*some*) locals don't like to say the word "no". It's considered rude to say no, so they say "yes". Even when they mean no. They don't feel it's rude to agree to do something and then not show up or follow through with their promises.

For some expats, that's going to both sound weird and feel frustrating. It's also not likely something you'll embrace and start doing to others.

And then there's Tico Time. Which, when you're on vacation here, probably got a few laughs.

When you live here, it can become annoying if you don't learn to just accept this as a part of the culture that you cannot change. Same with when someone tells you *mañana*, that could mean tomorrow, or sometime next week, next year or even... never.

> PRO TIP: You can't change a culture or people. You can only change how you react. And at some point, you may have to ask yourself:
>
> *Is getting frustrated over this really worth my time and energy?*

Nicknames

Where you come from, there may be sensitivities around calling people not-so-kind names, it might be considered insensitive and rude. Here, not so much.

For example, if you're skinny *flac@*, if you're overweight, *gord@*, if you're black, *negrit@*, etc.

The intention is not exactly one of malice. It's just how people get described here. Remember, *your* cultural lens may be different. You might consider saying that to someone, or being on the receiving end, very offensive. But here, that's not usually how it's meant.

Another question that I get asked is about the word gringa/gringo. *Is it a negative word?* It can be a way to describe a foreigner. I've known people from Argentina and other parts of the world who are called gring@s by locals, *it's not just directed at US citizens.*

Some people, however, don't really appreciate foreigners living in their country and it may be said in a negative way. Usually, you'll be able to figure out from the way it's being said, if it's a nickname for you or if it has a negative connotation.

The expectations of greetings

I annoyed a local friend because I didn't start every single conversation with a greeting. We were texting and talking every day. It just wasn't normal for me to say, "*good morning*" and "*how are you*" every single time we picked up the conversation.

But "normal" goes out the window when you're living in someone else's country. Their expectations and mannerisms are different.

By starting conversations with a greeting, it not only recognizes the presence and worth of the other individual but also sets a tone of respect and openness from the outset. Exchanging greetings is a way to commit to fostering positive energy each time you talk.

This is one of those things that I've adapted to, because it's not that hard to remember and a humble greeting can go a long way in creating connections and building bridges. Although sometimes I do still catch myself about to send a text and I realize I didn't start it off with, *Buenos días!*

Going to the hospital

It seems, based on my experience and what others have told me, a traditional custom here is to dress up when going to the hospital. Now, me, the very casual California girl, if I'm going to a hospital, it's because I'm really sick and likely the last thing I want to think about is putting on a dress and makeup, much less actually doing it. Even when I go to the EBAIS or a private clinic, that's not happening.

A local friend told me that when his girlfriend was giving birth, he was coming from the beach, wearing board shorts and a T-shirt and he was not permitted to enter. His home was over an hour away, so he had to find a nearby store and buy appropriate clothing.

Although, contrary to the custom of dressing up, you can't be *too* fancy, as I've seen visitors be told by the guards at the hospital and EBAIS clinics to remove their watches and their earrings before entering. (*I have no idea why...*)

"This is how it's always been done."

I've heard this a lot since moving here. Sometimes it's basic and doesn't really cause too much harm, other times it is indeed harmful, and can perpetuate stereotypes and discrimination as well as impede innovation and efficiency.

One example was a Tico friend wouldn't put toilet paper in the toilet, even though the pipes at my rental were able to handle the paper. He told me he didn't like to put it in the toilet, using the trash is "*how it's always been done*".

Another time, an ex of mine, many years ago, told me I was "*lazy*" because I used an electric toothbrush. He told me that a standard

Cultural Awareness & Adjustment

toothbrush is all that's needed, *this is how it's always been done*. He didn't want to hear that dentists recommend an electric toothbrush over a standard one, that it had been proven to be more effective and efficient. *No no*, I was simply *lazy* and that was that.

I want to mention here... I understand that possibly part of the issue was that he couldn't afford to buy an electric toothbrush, so it was easier for him to put it down, rather than have a curious mind and learn more about it.

> It's always a good idea to zoom out and see the big picture. To try to understand the "*why's*" behind the "*what's.*"

However, his reaction still wasn't appropriate (in my opinion). There are more mature ways to have a conversation. *Between his immaturity combined with his preference for watered down coffee, it became clear the relationship wouldn't last long.*

On the more damaging end of the spectrum, in the work I was doing when I first moved here, several men had made mistakes or failed to do their part of the project and when I asked them to fix the mistakes or do the work they were expected to do, I was told by the owner: *You can't tell the men they've made a mistake as it makes them feel bad. They also think you're bossy and arrogant.*

That's what misogyny looks like. When a woman can't speak up, be confident or be assertive in her role.

Sometimes, people are resistant to adopting new ways of doing things. This reluctance can often stem from a fear of the unknown or the uncertainty that change introduces into their lives, leading to concerns about how these changes will impact them.

They'd prefer to maintain the status quo than have to make shifts.

> But making those shifts and questioning the status quo... that is how progress happens and we can create a more open-minded and inclusive world.

I really didn't experience much sexism (or *"this is how it's always been done"*) while in the US, however I do recognize that it can happen anywhere. Since this was new for me, I wanted to include it here so that if it happens to you, you'll have a better cultural understanding of perhaps why it might be happening.

How to Find Common Ground

There may come a time when you want to share some of your own customs and beliefs with local friends that you meet.

So how do you educate others about your perspective and values without putting down an entire culture and history of tradition?

We can convey our perspective and values by following a few simple guidelines.

- ❖ Listen more than you speak. Take time to understand what people want and what they believe... versus what you think they *need*.
- ❖ Ask questions. Let them know you really want to learn and understand their perspective.
- ❖ Be respectful (in other words, don't call someone "*lazy*").
- ❖ Communicate calmly and clearly, using "I" statements when appropriate.
- ❖ Find common ground. Are there any areas where you agree? Be sure to highlight those.
- ❖ Know when to step away. To agree to disagree.

There may also be times when you really believe that something in the culture just doesn't feel right. For me, as an example, one thing is the abusive treatment of pets. And I have indeed been told: *This is just how it is here.*

Sometimes the only thing we can do is lead by example, and hope that others will learn from how we're choosing to show up in the world.

Having integrity, expressing empathy and being a responsible adult are some of the ways you can act as a role model.

You don't want to force your beliefs down someone else's throat, as doing so won't get you very far. Being respectful and mindfully choosing how you show up, for yourself and others, can begin to turn the tide and make a difference (*eventually*).

19

The Expat Experience

There's a whole chapter on how to *Be a Good Expat* but here I wanted to share a few notes about the expat experience.

Expat vs Immigrant

Let's talk about the terms expat and immigrant, which are often used interchangeably.

As you can see from this book, I mostly use expat, mainly because it's short, succinct and widely accepted.

And I happen to be a word nerd. I believe in the power of words (*and actions to accompany those words*) to transform and heal our world. And while I'm not perfect and I make mistakes, I do my best to be mindful of the words I use.

I also believe that how we define words can evolve with the times. Many words have changed their definitions throughout history.

Awful used to mean *full of awe*. Nice used to mean *foolish*. Hussy used to mean *housewife* and wench used to refer to a *female child*! Meat used to refer to all food, in general.

Let's look at the traditional definitions of expat and immigrant:

Expatriate (Expat): An expat typically refers to a person residing in a foreign country temporarily, often for work or education, with the intention of returning to their home country at some point. It could also mean they were exiled.

Immigrant: An immigrant, on the other hand, is someone who relocates to a new country with the intention of settling there permanently or for an extended period.

Personally, in my everyday life, I use both. I'm an "expat" who has expatriated from my home country to Costa Rica and I'm an immigrant living in Costa Rica. And while my intention is for Costa Rica to be my "forever home," I have learned *never to say never*.

So, is it okay to call oneself an expat? All things considered, you may have doubts regarding the appropriateness of identifying yourself as an "expat."

Here's a consideration for you: *Anyone who has left their home country can be an expat. Together, let's choose empathy and tolerance, recognizing the diversity of everyone's contributions (big or small) and work towards a world where all are accepted and valued, regardless of nationality or migration status.*

Redefining the term "expat" can be empowering for individuals, especially for those who often are labeled as immigrants in a negative way.

Acknowledging the privilege inherent in the term also opens up conversations about inequality, representation, and inclusivity within the global landscape.

Accepting the new normal.

In your home country, you may have lived on "auto-pilot." Everything ran smoothly. So smoothly, you may not have even realized how lucky you were.

ATM's always had money in them, bank lines weren't out the door, the electricity and internet were stable, water flowed freely from the faucet, the grocery store had every possible item you could ever imagine, you knew who you could trust and had a circle of people to give you solid referrals and support when needed. And that was just the tip of the iceberg.

Then you move to Costa Rica. And nothing is the same. You expected a peaceful, simple life but may end up feeling frustrated and disillusioned. "*Fed up*," as I've heard expressed by a lot of expats.

First, let me just say, if that's something you end up experiencing, it's normal. Some people deal with these things like water on a duck's back, it just doesn't bother them. But others may find it frustrating and inefficient.

Second, here are some everyday examples so that you can understand what causes those feelings of being "*fed up*" and help you prepare:

- Bureaucratic red tape
- Difficulty communicating and learning the language
- Financial strain
- Social isolation
- Healthcare concerns and difficulty accessing healthcare
- Culture shock and difficulty adjusting
- Long lines at banks, health care facilities and government offices

- Inconsistent internet service
- Power outages
- Understanding public transportation
- Struggling to find familiar products
- Dealing with currency exchange

Hopefully this book will help you figure out how to manage many of these!

Unmet expectations can also contribute to feelings of discontent among expats.

Expats may find themselves struggling with a sense of disconnect between the vision they had for their expat experience and the realities they encounter, fueling feelings of dissatisfaction.

I'm going to ask you to *please* remove your rose-colored glasses. It will make life so much easier if you live in reality versus a dream state.

It doesn't mean that everything is bad, simply that you recognize that there are challenges that come with living in what many consider a picture-perfect paradise.

And on that note…

I already talked about balancing a new culture with your own but here's something else you may experience... *People who shame others for maintaining traditions from their home country.* It seems crazy to me, but I've personally experienced it, and seen it happen to others.

What I'm talking about here concerns the traditions you do *privately*, in your home.

There's a difference between wanting to make a Thanksgiving meal in your home* and inviting friends... compared to expecting a local restaurant in Costa Rica to serve you a Thanksgiving meal (*although this doesn't mean you should expect to find everything you need to make the meal*).

Some people may feel threatened by cultural diversity and view the preservation of foreign traditions as a challenge to their own cultural norms. It disrupts their sense of familiarity and comfort.

A friendly reminder again that *some* Costa Ricans view foreigners living in their country in a negative light, and for many of the same reasons that *some* people in the US don't like people moving to their country.

As history has taught us, people who hold a strong sense of cultural superiority may look down upon the customs and cultures of others, considering them inferior.

Expats may be seen as disloyal to their adopted country if they choose to preserve their own cultural traditions and values.

There may be some people who believe that expats must assimilate completely and let go of their cultural identity. *Nationalism can fuel intolerance.*

Conformity as the only option may stem from a lack of exposure to other types of cultures and ways of being in the world. Ignorance and narrow-mindedness can lead to judgmental attitudes towards anything perceived as different or unfamiliar.

Use the tools that I gave in the Common Ground section to help you manage and overcome these perspectives.

Wanting a taste of home?

You may find yourself, one day, seeking out the familiar comforts of home, particularly when it comes to food. Which is completely normal and valid.

When I first moved and realized there were no *sour* yellow lemons, it was a very sad day.

Unfortunately, I've seen people shame others in Facebook groups because they were looking for comfort foods from home.

Comfort food, even if it's just a simple PB&J, can offer a sense of reassurance and stability in times of homesickness or loneliness and can provide a much-needed emotional boost.

Embracing food and culture from one's home country doesn't mean rejecting the offerings of Costa Rica. On the contrary, it's possible to celebrate both the familiar and the new together.

Sharing meals and traditions from your home country can serve as a bridge to connect with locals.

Root beer was a rare find here many years ago but when I did finally find it, I brought home a bottle and made a Root Beer Float for a local friend. He had never had one before and loved it.

That said, introducing new foods isn't always appreciated. When I first moved here, I invited a few friends over for dinner. I made one of my favorites, a spinach and polenta dish. Only my Italian friend liked it. Change takes time and I was grateful that my local friends at least tried the meal.

The "ungrateful foreigner" stereotype

I've been in situations where expressing frustration can feel like breaking some unwritten rule of expat etiquette.

Take, for example, the everyday struggles of managing bureaucracy in Costa Rica.

Trying to renew your residency or get your driver's license can feel like running a marathon through a maze - frustrating, time-consuming, and often confusing. But dare to complain about it, and you might be met with raised eyebrows and a well-meaning reminder to "*just relax, it's pura vida, mae.*"

Then there's the language barrier. Sure, you might have mastered the basics of Spanish before moving to Costa Rica, but that doesn't mean you're fluent overnight.

Miscommunications are bound to happen. But admitting that you're struggling with the language? Cue the judgmental stares and whispers about how you should have learned Spanish before coming here.

Or imagine you're at a get together and someone asks how you're adjusting.

You want to be real, to admit that some days feel more like a ride on a rollercoaster than a siesta in a hammock. But you hesitate, knowing that expressing anything less than "pura vida" might earn you a label as the "ungrateful foreigner."

And let's not forget about the pressure to maintain a picture-perfect image on social media. Behind the filters and #iliveinparadise hashtags lies a more challenging reality.

Some days, you might feel lost, alone and really uncomfortable. But sharing those feelings online might not be received well, inviting judgment or criticism from those who believe you should be nothing but grateful for your tropical surroundings.

The stereotype of the ungrateful foreigner in Costa Rica stems from a narrow-minded idea of expat life, one that prioritizes positivity (*which too much can actually be toxic!*) and ignores the complexities of real-life experiences.

People – locals, other expats and your friends from your home country – may pressure you to feel like everything always has to be perfect.

But by accepting the messy, imperfect reality of expat life, we create space for genuine connection, compassion, and understanding.

Let's ditch the stereotype and be open to the full spectrum of expat emotions (*which we'll review in the chapter on Mental Health*), from the highs to the lows and everything in between.

Because when we allow ourselves to be vulnerable and honest about our experiences, we invite others to do the same, fostering a community of kindness, built on authenticity and empathy.

Let's keep my mantra on repeat please: *Less judgment. More compassion.*

20

Mental Health

Like any major life change, living in Costa Rica can bring about negative feelings or challenges. I can't stress enough that having a solid support system is imperative, especially if you arrive here already struggling with a mental health condition.

While Costa Rica can alleviate many of the stresses and anxiety that you feel in your home country, it can also exacerbate mental health issues (*and bring on new ones*) if you don't have a solid plan on how to manage challenges when they arise.

Real talk... I have known a few people here who really struggled with mental health issues and/or substance abuse issues. If you arrive with those difficulties, Costa Rica will likely not be a cure, and it could even make things worse. Sadly, I've known quite a few people who died of a drug overdose or committed suicide.

Alcohol and drugs are prevalent in communities around the country. But the good news is, there are also AA and NA meetings in many towns. And nowadays, you can often find therapy via online sources.

Even if you don't currently have mental health struggles, please ensure you have people who you can turn to, when things go awry.

How to deal with uncertain times

I know the thought of living in Costa Rica is exciting but I'm going to ask you to acknowledge that there is also an inherent unpredictability that comes with moving abroad. The many twists and turns of expat life requires resilience, adaptability, and a realistic mindset.

One of the first lessons you need to learn is to accept uncertainty. No matter how meticulously you may plan, unforeseen circumstances are bound to arise. Managing them requires an openness to let go of control and adjust to the unexpected.

Then, build up that resilience muscle.

I would say resilience is a cornerstone of my life here, bouncing forward from setbacks (*not back...*

as who wants to go back to the place where they were before!), whether they were minor inconveniences or major obstacles. You will likely be faced with unfamiliar challenges and developing a mindset of resilience will help you persevere through tough times.

Next, take off those rose-colored glasses.

Contrary to what some people believe, being a realist doesn't mean being negative. It does, however, give you a more accurate understanding of the many types of experiences you will have here, helping you manage daily life more effectively.

It also enables you to manage your expectations, as living abroad often involves encountering differences from your home country. A realistic mindset allows you to adapt more readily to these changes and avoid unnecessary frustration or disappointment.

It can also help you make informed decisions, ensuring your well-being and safety while living in Costa Rica.

Bend. Don't break.

Plans may change at a moment's notice, whether due to unforeseen circumstances or cultural norms. Learning to adapt and go with the flow can help to alleviate the stress you may be feeling when life throws you a curve ball.

Lastly, celebrate the small wins.

Take time to celebrate when things go well. Whether it's finally being able to correctly say "guanabana," getting from Point A to Point B in the public transportation system without getting lost, or submitting all the necessary paperwork for your residency application, acknowledging these accomplishments can boost your spirit and provide motivation during challenging times.

Now let's explore the common feelings many expats feel as they adjust to living here (and even many years into living here):

Naming our feelings is essential for emotional clarity, which enhances self-awareness and can improve the expat experience. Understanding what the feeling is, and where it comes from, can help create healthier relationships (*with yourself and others*) and improve your decision-making skills.

Frustration: Dealing with bureaucracy, cultural differences, or language barriers.

Isolation and Alienation: Feeling disconnected from friends, family, or social support networks back home or feeling like an outsider, struggling to connect with people in your community.

Anxiety and Insecurity: Concerns about finances, job stability, healthcare, or safety. Feeling uncertain about the future and whether you're making the right choices.

Loneliness: Missing loved ones or struggling to make meaningful connections in a new environment.

Stress: Managing the challenges of daily life in a new country, such as finding housing or adapting to a new culture, can be stressful.

Discontentment: Feeling dissatisfied with aspects of life in Costa Rica, such as the weather, infrastructure, or cultural differences.

Exhaustion: You may have a list of five things to do in one day, but you only end up accomplishing two... *because things are different here.*

Regret: Questioning whether moving to Costa Rica was the right decision or feeling regretful about leaving behind the comforts of home.

That's a pressure cooker of feelings! And as I mentioned in the Ungrateful Foreigner section, in societies all around the world including in Costa Rica, expressing negative feelings is often looked down upon (*thankfully, that's slowly changing*).

Just as a pressure cooker needs to release steam to prevent an explosion, you need to release pent-up emotions to prevent emotional buildup and alleviate stress.

By giving voice to your feelings and what you're experiencing, you allow yourself to let go of internal tension, which can lead to feeling relieved and a sense of calm.

> It's okay to admit when things aren't going well and seek help.

But what do you do when everything is going wrong (and trust me, it can happen!)?

When faced with a string of setbacks or when the world seems to be crashing down around you, it can feel really overwhelming. *Adulting can be hard, even in your home country!* Remember that challenges are an inevitable part of life, especially when you're leaping into a new country, culture, and way of life.

Take a step back. When life starts to unravel, it's easy to feel overwhelmed, to let panic take over.

Take a moment to breathe and distance yourself from the situation. Shift gears, go out for a walk, or do something to help you take your mind off it, so you can return to the situation later with fresh eyes and a clear mind.

Break down the problem. Sometimes, it might seem like everything is falling apart at once, making it difficult to pinpoint the exact issues at hand. Is it a personal problem, a cultural misunderstanding, or a logistical issue?

Understanding the root cause will help you not only determine what steps need to be taken but also what kind of support you need. Take the time to break down the problem into smaller, more manageable parts. Then handle each of those, one at a time.

Ask for help. Don't hesitate to reach out and ask for support. Friends and family members might offer advice or perspectives that you hadn't considered.

When seeking support... Consider framing your request in a way that emphasizes your need for empathy and understanding. Instead of simply venting about your problems, express your desire to share your feelings in a safe and non-judgmental environment.

For example, you could say, *"I've been having a tough time lately, and I could really use someone to talk to. Can we chat over coffee?"*

Additionally, it may be helpful to set boundaries around the type of support you're seeking. If you're *not* looking for advice or solutions but simply need a listening ear, make that clear to your friends and family.

By communicating your needs openly and honestly, you can help ensure that your support system respects your boundaries and provides the kind of assistance you're looking for.

Consult experts. If you decide the problem is more in-depth than friends or family can help with, consult professionals such as attorneys, accountants, or relocation specialists/life abroad mentors (*Hello, have we met? I'm Chrissy, your Costa Rica Expat Expert ;)*). They can provide personalized advice, services and resources for your situation and help you manage the challenges you face.

Practice patience. Dealing with challenges in a foreign country can be frustrating and time-consuming. Solutions may not always come quickly, so practice patience.

Learn from the experience: Every challenge presents an opportunity for growth and learning.

Reflect on what went wrong and what you could do differently in the future. See setbacks as stepping stones to whatever comes next on your expat journey.

Express gratitude: If I may get a little woo-woo here, *it's important for expats to maintain not only a realistic perspective but also a sense of gratitude.*

While I want you to be realistic, I also want you to recognize that living in Costa Rica is a privilege, and there is so much beauty and wonder to be found in every corner of this extraordinary country.

Take the time to appreciate the little things... the sound of waves crashing against the shore, the warmth of the sunshine and the freshness of a tropical storm. Or whatever it may be that brings *you* a sense of joy and creates calm in your life.

Lastly, please remember, you have the strength and resources within you to overcome any obstacle that comes your way. And I'm right here, (*virtually*) by your side, cheering you on.

21

Personal Relations

When your friends and family aren't supportive of your move

You've planned an amazing get together with all your friends and family, and when you announce the big news that you're moving, the response you receive is less than celebratory and congratulatory. It happens a lot more frequently than you might imagine.

When faced with unsupportive friends and family, the excitement of moving abroad can quickly become overshadowed by feelings of frustration and isolation.

Although we often look for approval and support from those nearest to us, it's important to keep in mind that not everyone will understand or agree with our decisions.

If friends or family aren't supportive of your move, here's some ideas on how to manage that:

Keep the doors of communication open. Set aside time to sit down with them and explain your reasons for wanting to move to Costa Rica. Encourage them to express their concerns and actively listen... *without becoming defensive.*

Educate them. Lack of support can stem from misconceptions about Costa Rica. Educate your friends and family about the country – its culture, lifestyle, and the reasons why you want to call this country, "*home.*" You can highlight the potential problems but also let them know you're aware no place is perfect and you're prepared to manage the challenges.

Empathy and understanding. Reassure them and try to empathize with your loved ones' concerns and fears about your move. Recognize that their concerns may come from fear of losing you or worries about your safety.

Setting boundaries. If they continue to be unsupportive, set some boundaries. Respectfully let them know that while you value their opinions, the decision to move is ultimately yours, and you hope they can respect that. And then seek support elsewhere.

Give it time. Be patient with your friends and family and give them space to come to terms with your decision. Hopefully, eventually, they'll come around.

How to make friends

For some people, making friends is easy peasy. But, for those of you who have spent many years in one location, cultivating friendships that span decades, or for those who are naturally more introverted, the task of making new friends can be particularly intimidating, especially when you're in a new culture and country.

Hello, my name is... Introduce yourself to your neighbors. Express your interest in getting to know them. And once you're settled in, remember what it was like to be new and take the initiative to meet neighbors when they move in. Become the welcoming committee.

Be friendly. Smile, wave, and be courteous whenever you see your neighbors. Small gestures can go a long way in breaking down barriers.

Attend community events. Make an effort to attend community events, so you can meet your neighbors in a more relaxed setting.

Acts of kindness. If you notice a neighbor struggling with something, offer to help.

Shared interests. Build connections by finding common ground. Love gardening? Painting? Kayaking? Look for others who are into the same types of hobbies you enjoy.

Volunteer. Give back to the community and connect with people who are interested in the same things as you.

Language exchange meetups. Some towns have language exchange meetups where locals and expats come together to practice speaking different languages.

Be patient. Making friends, especially ones that are genuine and long-lasting, takes time. Practice patience. Keep putting yourself out there and eventually, you'll find your people.

You're not going to like everyone

As someone who was an extrovert in California and always the party planner, easily making friends with most everyone I met, moving here was a little different.

My first group of friends here, while they were super friendly and helpful people, their lifestyle just didn't align with my own.

But not everyone I've met has been friendly or helpful. Post sepsis, I have to be hypervigilant regarding my health (*these days I freak out over the smallest scratch or a bug bite*). When my car was in the shop for a week, I reached out to a couple who I thought were friends and asked them... "*If I have an emergency this week, can I reach out to you for help*"?

The response received was not what I was expecting. That they, a retired couple, had errands to run around town so I couldn't count on them to help. I didn't expect them to drop everything, I just wanted to know that I could reach out to someone who could maybe help me figure out how to get to the hospital.

Think about the town where you're from... some people may have been your closest friends, while there were others you chose not to associate with or didn't even know, especially if your town had more than a few thousand people.

Here, it's often on a much smaller scale, so everyone knows everyone. That has its upsides... and its downsides.

You need to decide who do you want in your life? What are your non-negotiables when it comes to the types of people you want to associate with and call your friends? Are you comfortable being on your own for a while as you figure those things out and look for the right people?

The revolving expat door

In my first year or two of living here, a few seasoned expats shared their reluctance to befriend newcomers, explaining that many new expats often leave after a short period.

They didn't want to invest the time and energy in developing a friendship and then the next thing they knew, their new friends decide Costa Rica is not for them and leave.

I had a hard time with that. I could take a step back and see their point, but it was a new reality that I had to let sink in.

Of course, *not everyone* feels this way but it's something to be aware of, if you find yourself struggling to connect with others.

As a newcomer, be humble and grateful...

Those seasoned expats also shared with me that sometimes newcomers arrive with too much ego and not enough humility, and they just didn't want to be around that type of person.

I had my own experience of that recently and looking back at what they had said, I could understand their rationale.

Recently, I shared the contact information of a reputable service provider with a newcomer, someone I thought I was becoming friends with. I told her at the time that I had previously interviewed five people before finally finding a sixth who was competent. The extensive search process drained a lot of energy and even led to some wasted money, as I had mistakenly hired the wrong person initially.

Not only did she not give a polite response of *thank you*, but she also, later, took credit for finding them. Blatantly disregarding the time and effort it took me to find that person.

Seasoned expats can provide you with a wealth of information.

If they choose to share their knowledge with you, be humble, kind and grateful, remembering just how much they have possibly had to endure and experience to get them to where they are today.

22

Language Tips

Learning to speak Spanish is an absolute necessity for moving to Costa Rica. Some people may disagree, saying you can get by without knowing the language, but it really will make your life, and your time here on the Rich Coast, so much easier. Plus, it's a way of showing respect to your newly adopted country.

Take classes. Before moving, enroll in Spanish classes either in-person or online. Look for reputable language schools, community colleges, or online apps like Duolingo or Rosetta Stone.

Practice regularly. Consistent practice is key to learning the language. Set aside dedicated time each day to practice speaking, listening, reading, and writing in Spanish. A study group can not only support you in learning the language but also help you make friends.

Immerse yourself. Immerse yourself with the language as much as possible. Listen to Spanish music, watch Spanish movies and TV shows, and try to engage in conversations with Spanish speakers.

Read in Spanish. Start with simple texts like children's books, news articles, or blogs written in Spanish. Gradually progress to more complex materials as your proficiency increases.

Watch TV in Spanish. Set your subtitles to English so you understand what they're saying. You'll be surprised how much comprehension you can pick up this way! Or, if you want to get better at reading and recognizing words, do the reverse and set your subtitles to Spanish.

Online Resources: Explore online resources such as YouTube channels, podcasts, and language learning websites.

Practice patience: Learning a new language takes time and effort. Stay motivated, set achievable goals, and celebrate your progress along the way.

I remember when I finally didn't have to say, "*please slow down*." I actually understood what the person was saying the first time he spoke it and I then realized how much more at ease and confident I felt!

> True story: About 3 years into living here, I went to the doctor, and I was still very shy about speaking Spanish. As I was going in, an expat was leaving. When I met with the doctor, I apologized for my bad Spanish, and she replied:
>
> *"Did you see that man who just left? He's lived here for 10 years and can't speak any Spanish. Your Spanish is very good!"*
>
> Don't be that man. Do your best to integrate and learn the language!

Language etiquette

I took Spanish classes while still living in California. My teacher, who was amazing, taught "Mexican" Spanish. At the time, I didn't realize there was a difference.

Until I moved to Costa Rica.

In Spanish, the use of different forms of address, such as "tú," "usted," and "vos," can vary.

Costa Rica is <u>super formal</u> when it comes to language. Way more formal than I personally like but I accept that this is how it is here.

"Usted" is generally considered more formal and respectful than "tú." Using "usted" is a way to show politeness and respect, particularly when speaking to someone older or in a position of authority.

While the use of "tú" is not unheard of in Costa Rica, particularly among youth and in very casual contexts, the use of "usted" and "vos" reflects cultural norms of respect, courtesy, and tradition; even with loved ones, for some locals.

Words that look alike in Spanish and English but have different meanings!

A similar-looking word in English might carry a vastly different meaning in Spanish, leading to potential confusion or embarrassment if not used correctly.

"Embarazada" and "Embarrassed": This is the classic example where "embarazada" means "pregnant" in Spanish, but "embarrassed" in English.

"Sopa" and "Soap": "Sopa" means "soup" in Spanish, while "soap" refers to a cleaning product.

"Exit" and "Éxito": In English, "exit" means a way out, while "éxito" in Spanish means "success."

Excitado does not mean excited. Well, it kinda does but not in the way you may be thinking. Excitado means more like "aroused" whereas emocionado means excited.

"Molestar" and "Molest": "Molestar" means "to bother" or "to annoy" in Spanish, while "molest" means to sexually abuse in English.

"Pie". In Spanish, "pie" means "foot," while in English, it refers to a dessert.

"Ropa" and "Rope": "Ropa" means "clothing" in Spanish, while "rope" refers to a thick cord.

"Carpeta" and "Carpet": "Carpeta" in Spanish usually means "folder" or "file," while "carpet" in English refers to a floor covering.

"Library" and "Librería": In English, "library" refers to a place where books are kept and loaned out, while "librería" in Spanish means a bookstore or shop, where you can find odds and ends like pens and paper as well as a place to get copies made.

"Largo" and "Large": "Largo" in Spanish means "long," while "large" in English means big or spacious.

"Sensible": In English, "sensible" means having or showing good sense or judgment, while in

Spanish, it can mean sensitive or sensible, depending on the context.

And a note about accents...

Be mindful when writing Spanish words with accents to avoid mistakes... For example, omitting the accent in "año" turns it into a different word, "ano."

The word "año" means "year." However, if you miss the tilde over the 'n' (ñ), you get "ano," which translates to "anus" in English. (*whoops!*)

23

Expressions

I don't use a lot of slang (*even in English*) but there are some people who will tell you that if you don't learn and use *Pachuco (Spanish slang specific to Costa Rica)*, you'll never integrate into Costa Rica society (*I disagree*).

That said, here are a few:

- Mae – Slang for "dude"
- Tuanis – cool, nice, usually referencing a person
- Que chiva – cool! (In Spanish, it actually means "goat")
- Brete – Work or a job
- Birra – Beer
- Goma – Hangover (actually means "glue")
- Solo bueno – only good
- Plata – money

And we all know "pura vida" right?

Expressions

"Pura vida" is the official slogan of Costa Rica that translates to "pure life" or "simple life." While it generally conveys positivity and an easygoing attitude, there are some potential problems associated with the concept. I write more about this in my book, *Lost and Found in the Land of Mañana,* but to quickly review some of the highlights to take into consideration:

The phrase can sometimes be used as a way of ignoring or downplaying real challenges or hardships.

A few years ago, I was waiting in line to get meds at the EBAIS pharmacy, and an older man started to chat with me. He told me how he had been waiting over a year to get medical care for a problem with his elbow. He had an *extremely* large growth, which he told me was very uncomfortable in his day-to-day life.

He told me that he was a farmer and how it was difficult to maintain his land in his condition. He then shrugged his shoulders and said, in a frustrated and sarcastic tone, "*pura vida*", and went on to explain how this mentality of "pure life" creates disillusionment. That everyone keeps saying the phrase but for many people here, it isn't reality because of all the challenges they face.

And he's not the first (*or last*) Tic@ to use the expression in a sarcastic tone.

> Through conversations with local friends and random strangers, we can begin to peel back the layers and gain a more holistic understanding of our adopted country. We come to realize that not everything is entirely good or bad; instead, we can accept the existence of a complex, messy middle.

Emphasizing "pura vida" not only discourages critical thinking and proactive problem-solving, but it can also minimize societal problems and encourage a mindset of complacency and a lack of motivation for improvement or progress. Not just for individuals and their own personal growth but collectively as well, for the society as a whole.

While "pura vida" is generally seen as a positive and uplifting concept, I'd ask you to recognize its limitations and potential downsides, especially when it's used without consideration for the complexities of life.

"Dura vida" as a variation of "pura vida"

Some people might use the term "dura vida" sarcastically as a play on words of "pura vida." The word "duro" in Spanish means "hard" so "dura vida" could be interpreted as "hard life."

Expats might use it to convey a different perspective on their experiences living in a foreign country and acknowledge the challenges and frustrations they come across while adapting to a new country, culture and language.

But "dura vida" may not be universally understood or appreciated, especially if it's perceived as mocking the positive connotations of "pura vida."

Take into consideration cultural sensitivity and how the phrase might be received by local speakers or others in the expat community.

(these days, personally, I don't use either…)

Siempre hay algo /

"There's always something." This casual expression is often used in conversations to convey a relentless series of challenges, without sharing much detail about what's going on.

I heard (*and said*) these expressions so often here that I once jokingly told a Nicaraguan friend that I'd someday write a book with that title (*and I did…*).

Si dios quiere

Another common expression here, one I've literally heard thousands of times – probably even more than pura vida, is "*if god wants*". If god wants, I'll be there tomorrow. If god wants, the store will have the pet food. If god wants, I'll meet you for dinner.

"*Así es la vida*"

A phrase said in moments of despair or declared with a shrug of resignation. A phrase I've said a lot since moving to the Rich Coast. It's a succinct summary of our everyday experiences, meaning "such is life."

It reflects how our lives are unpredictable, filled with twists and turns, wins and losses, 10,000 joys and 10,000 sorrows. It embodies the acceptance of impermanence and change.

It reminds us that life isn't always fair or kind and to adapt and persevere in the face of adversity. It teaches us humility and encourages us to surrender to the flow of life, rather than futilely resisting its currents.

Expressions

It's not just the Spanish language that has such a phrase (*although I do use it way more here than I ever did in the US!*)

I took French in high school, so I knew this one: *"C'est la vie."* And a German friend here told me: "So ist das leben," is the expression in Germany.

In English: "That's life," "It is what it is," "Such is life," "That's how the cookie crumbles."

"Que sera, sera": I always thought this was French but, in my research, it doesn't seem to have an exact country of origin and could be from Spanish, French or Italian origin. It translates to "*Whatever will be, will be.*"

"Ahorita or Ahora"

There are many jokes about this word's meaning. It means "right now" or "very soon," but it can also be used as "a little while later" or "later" in other circumstances, leading to misunderstandings and sometimes, frustration.

24

Fun. Interesting. Random

In this chapter are all the many things that I couldn't find a suitable place to put elsewhere, but still wanted to share with you. They're fun, interesting, random and in no particular order!

Let me introduce you to the mythical rain bird.

That's what I call him at least. He sings his sweet song announcing the end of summer and rain is on the horizon. All around the country, but even more so for those of us who live in coastal areas, we're doing happy dances when we hear him.

It also happens to be the national bird. Its real name is clay-colored thrush or *yigüirro*.

Other national symbols include the white-tailed deer, an orchid, the decorative ox cart, the Guanacaste tree, the Marimba and most recently, the sloth.

Fun. Interesting. Random.

The flag

The national flag consists of five horizontal stripes: blue, white, red, white, and blue. From what I've read, the blue color represents the sky, as well as opportunities, perseverance, and the ideals of the Costa Rican citizens. The white color symbolizes peace, wisdom, and happiness. The red color represents the blood shed for freedom and the warmth of the Costa Rican people.

First female president

Laura Chinchilla was president of Costa Rica from 2010-2014. She had previously served as Vice-President, Congresswoman and Minister of Security and Justice. She graduated from the University of Costa Rica with a degree in Political Science and received a master's degree in Public Policy from Georgetown University, in Washington D.C., United States. She is a member of the PLN party (*political party information is provided in the Government chapter*).

Religion

Stats I've found say that about 75% of the population is Catholic, 15% are protestant or evangelical, and the remaining are other Christan denominations like Jehovah's Witnesses. A very small percentage are agnostic, atheist, Quaker, Jewish, Muslim or Buddhist.

Paying Bills

If you're responsible for paying for utilities, Caja, property taxes or other bills associated with a government agency, there are a few ways to do so. You will need to know the number associated with the account.

If you don't have a local bank account, you can pay many of those types of bills at local supermarkets. If you have a local bank account, you can pay by going into the bank or using their online platform. Some companies will offer the option to pay in person or via SINPE.

> NOTE: You might not always receive a bill. You are still responsible to pay and oftentimes, there is no grace period. *i.e.* your electricity will be turned off the day after the bill is due!

Toothpaste

I was a Tom's of Maine user in the US but coming here, I've had to adjust. It's only been in recent years that it was easy to find a few other brands, besides Colgate. Before, you'd be lucky if you could find 2-3 boxes of Sensodyne and the occasional Crest. Now you can find a few more options in the toothpaste aisle as long as you can get past the 1,000 boxes of Colgate.

I now get toothpaste in bulk that I buy from Amazon. Not super easy or cheap to get it here but I prefer to use products with less chemicals. And that's been hard to find here.

Peanut butter

Most Tic@s didn't grow up eating PB&J sandwiches. Peanut butter is imported so it's pricey. These days, I make my own. Super easy. I have a very small, but very powerful food processor and in just a few minutes, I have perfect peanut butter. I buy the peanuts at Pricesmart.

But before, I was buying Jif (*I was a Skippy girl growing up*) and the prices were just ridiculous. One time many years ago, I did actually find Skippy... it was $13 for a small jar.

Trees

When thinking about Costa Rica, you likely conjure up the image of palm trees, but did you know that there are places around the country that have both pine trees and oak trees?

If you're originally from an area that has those, know that on the days when you may be feeling a little homesick, you can always venture into the mountains and find a "comfort tree" to hug.

We don't change our clocks!

Okay who just stood up and did a happy dance? Yep, you read that right, since we're so close to the equator, there isn't a need to change our clocks. Sunrise is generally between 5am and 6am and sunset is between 5pm and 6pm. ALL YEAR LONG. One thing to consider however is that means no late nights when it's still sunny at 8 or 9pm. And for some people, that can be a really hard adjustment.

Costa Rica, a small but big country!

The population here is around 5.2 million people (2024). The size of Costa Rica is 19,730 square miles. For comparison, the closest US state in size would be West Virginia which is about 24,000 square miles. Yet West Virginia only has about 1.8 million people.

Fun. Interesting. Random.

Dates and months

January 7th in the US would be written as 1-7 whereas in Costa Rica (*and much of the rest of the world*), it would be 7-1. Also, words that are capitalized in English, like months, are not capitalized in Spanish. So, March would be written marzo. Other words not capitalized include nationalities, days of the week, languages and "I" (*yo*).

The Great Egg Debate

In many countries outside of the United States, eggs are not typically refrigerated. But if you're coming from the US, that might seem strange.

In the US, eggs are washed before they are sold. This washing process removes not just the dirt, debris and possible salmonella, it also removes the outer protective layer of the shell called the bloom, which helps to prevent bacteria from entering the egg. However, refrigeration then becomes necessary to inhibit bacterial growth and maintain freshness.

For the greater good

When the pandemic shut everything down, the government had said they'd raise taxes on people who earned over a certain amount (*I think it was* *around $2,500/*month) in order to help out those people who were no longer working.

When I asked some local friends about that, who weren't wealthy but were in that tax bracket, they all said: *Of course, we must help each other out during this difficult time.* When it comes to raising taxes, that is not the kind of response you'd hear from a lot of people in the US...

Smoke Detectors

Out of the seventeen rentals that I've lived in, only ONE has had a smoke detector and even more randomly, it was in the master bedroom. You'd think if there was one in the bedroom, there'd be one in the kitchen, but there was not.

A win for the animals

Hunting is illegal here. Circuses are not allowed to use animals in their performances. Some zoos are closing up shop. Keeping a wild animal as a pet is illegal and there's even a campaign to stop people from taking selfies with wild animals. Touching or feeding wild animals is illegal. If you see a wild animal in distress, contact MINAE or a local wildlife protection organization in your area. (*Your local Facebook group will usually be the best place to find those organizations.*)

The lack of yellow lemons

It's only been recently that yellow lemons of the acidic variety have started to pop up a bit more frequently in grocery stores. But still, it's not a regular occurrence, at least not where I live. You'll find many varieties of green limes and sweet yellow lemons, but *sour* yellow lemons are still rare in 2024. When you do find them, you'll likely pay around $1 for each.

Food storage

If you're in a particularly humid environment, or have problems with pantry moths, you'll want to consider putting dried herbs and spices in the fridge. Pasta, grains, nuts, seeds and flour can be kept in the freezer.

Unplug it!

Depending on your location, the power might pop on and off quite a lot. Like multiple times each day. Today alone, my power has popped off and on at least fifteen times.

Not only do I recommend battery backups but when you're not using certain items (*like the blender, toaster oven, washer, dryer, etc*), keep them unplugged. Those constant blips of power surges can often lead to damaged devices.

The many Playa Hermosas

I know of four "beautiful beaches," as it translates to English, in Costa Rica, but I've heard there are at least five.

- Playa Hermosa, near Playas del Coco
- Playa Hermosa, near Jacó
- Playa Hermosa, Uvita
- Playa Hermosa, Santa Teresa

I haven't been able to find the fifth...

There are also at least three Playa Matapalo's. When you're talking about location here, be sure to include additional reference points, the province or a larger town nearby.

ICE

Newcomers who aren't familiar with Spanish often call the national electric company's abbreviated name like how you'd say *ice*, the frozen water that quickly melts in a power outage here.

But actually... ICE (Instituto Costarricense de Electricidad/Costa Rican Institute of Electricity) is pronounced E-Say. Because I sounds like e and E sounds like a. Now you know!

And on that topic, in most cases, I'd recommend getting a Kolbi sim. As it's the national mobile phone company, associated with ICE, I've found it really does have the best coverage nationwide.

Roaming is also available if you set up international calling before you leave the country. If you can also get fiber optic from ICE, it is often a better deal than other fiber optic companies in the country.

Prostitution

Prostitution is legal. However, brothels are illegal. Which, as I took a moment to think that through… while I suppose it empowers the woman to be an entrepreneur, at the same time, a brothel can provide a safe place when working in a risky business.

The death penalty

During my research, I found three different years, so to be as accurate as possible, I'll simply state that it was abolished in the late 19th century.

The land of peace

We have no military here! I know, I've said that elsewhere in the book, but it's worth repeating.

25

Legal Matters

Why hire an attorney?

Attorneys are hired here for reasons that might seem strange to those of us from other countries. For example, buying a car.

An attorney can help you understand and obey the many laws and steps you need to take to protect yourself, whether you're starting a business, purchasing property, or dealing with government agencies.

If you're entering into contracts or agreements, having an attorney review and negotiate the terms can help safeguard your interests and ensure that you fully understand your rights and responsibilities.

Instead of using a title company when purchasing a property, here we use attorneys. Buying or selling property here can be complex, especially for foreigners. An attorney can assist with due diligence, title searches, drafting purchase agreements, and any other legal issues that may arise during the transaction.

If you're planning to obtain residency, an attorney can guide you through the immigration process, helping you understand the different options available and ensuring that you meet all requirements as well as filing all the necessary paperwork, securing an appointment for you, and walking you through the process.

An attorney can help you with all the necessary paperwork to open a business. You can open a business without residency, but you need *permanent residency* in order to work for the business. Without it, you need to hire locals.

Labor Laws Snapshot

Please hire an attorney to understand labor laws in Costa Rica when hiring individuals to work, even for domestic tasks. Even if it's just once a week, for 2 hours.

In general, Costa Rica is considered to be more employee-friendly than business-friendly. There are steps that need to be taken to ensure both your day-to-day obligations to the employee or contractor are met as well as if you terminate your working agreement with them or they quit.

If you don't set it up correctly from the start, you may be liable for a lot more money than you originally thought you'd be paying the person.

Festive cheer brought to you by the Aguinaldo

I only ever worked for one company that gave holiday bonuses while in the US.

But in Costa Rica, every worker receives one!

NB: Some people get upset when it's called a "bonus" but for those of us coming from a place like the US, "bonus" is an easy term to identify with, understand and use.

The "aguinaldo" is a mandatory annual payment, paid to employees by their employers in the month of December, often called the "13th" month of salary. The aguinaldo is calculated based on the total salary earned by the employee throughout the year.

The aguinaldo is an important source of income for many Costa Rican workers during the holiday season, helping them cover expenses and participate in the festivities.

26

The Government

Political Parties

Some of you might find this odd, but I would characterize Costa Rica as a *"conservative country with socialist ideals."*

Now, if you're from the US, that might have you tilting your head to one side and thinking *"How can that be??"*

Because of the Catholic Church, and the majority of people here being either Catholic or Christian, this is a VERY conservative country. However, there are also socialist ideals in place like free education, healthcare for all, and no military.

Liberals who come here might think that with the laidback lifestyle and all the social welfare programs, that must mean the country is more progressive.

Conservatives who come here might think that since the country is so conservative with abortion being illegal and "traditional" values, that must mean the country has a mentality of small government and "each (hu)man for themselves." That is very much not the case either.

In my experience, the citizens here (*not all, but many*) are peaceful, non-confrontational, and are more inclined to do what the government tells them versus make their own personal choices. It is, after all, a society that values collectivism over capitalism and individuality. That said, there are protests here, usually related to transportation, teachers, or taxes.

As far as the government being involved, I've known people who had the police and the health department (or, depending on the situation, PANI – the National Institute for Children) show up at their door because their children were not vaccinated according to the required schedule. The government will also administer vaccines at schools, without parental consent.

Vaccines are SUPER important here, including controversial ones like the HPV vaccine which is required for girls (*not boys*) at age 10 (2024). Costa Ricans are immensely proud of how they were able to eradicate diseases through the use of vaccines.

Political parties

National Liberation Party (Partido Liberación Nacional, PLN): One of the oldest political parties in Costa Rica. Associated with centrist and social democratic policies.

Social Christian Unity Party (Partido Unidad Social Cristiana, PUSC): Another long-standing party, typically associated with center-right policies. It is based in Christianity.

Citizen Action Party (Partido Acción Ciudadana, PAC): Founded in the early 2000s, PAC is a progressive party that advocates for transparency, anti-corruption, and social justice.

National Restoration Party (Partido Restauración Nacional, PRN): PRN is a conservative party which values Christian ideals and traditions.

Broad Front (Frente Amplio): Liberal party that advocates for environmental sustainability, social justice, and human rights.

Costa Rican Renovation Party (Partido Renovación Costarricense, PRC): A conversative party with fundamentalist views on social and economic issues.

Accessibility Without Exclusion Party (Partido Accesibilidad Sin Exclusión, PASE): Advocates for the rights of people with disabilities, promoting accessibility and inclusion.

Government agencies

- Ministry of the Presidency (Ministerio de la Presidencia)
- Ministry of Foreign Affairs and Worship (Ministerio de Relaciones Exteriores y Culto)
- Ministry of Finance (Ministerio de Hacienda)
- Ministry of Public Education (Ministerio de Educación Pública)
- Ministry of Health (Ministerio de Salud)
- Ministry of Labor and Social Security (Ministerio de Trabajo y Seguridad Social)
- Ministry of Environment and Energy (Ministerio de Ambiente y Energía - MINAE)
- Ministry of Agriculture and Livestock (Ministerio de Agricultura y Ganadería)
- Ministry of Economy, Industry, and Commerce (Ministerio de Economía, Industria y Comercio)
- Ministry of Public Security (Ministerio de Seguridad Pública)

- Ministry of Transportation and Public Works (Ministerio de Obras Públicas y Transportes)
- Ministry of Culture and Youth (Ministerio de Cultura y Juventud)
- Ministry of Housing and Human Settlements (Ministerio de Vivienda y Asentamientos Humanos)
- Ministry of Justice and Peace (Ministerio de Justicia y Paz)
- Ministry of Planning and Economic Policy (Ministerio de Planificación Nacional y Política Económica)

A special shout out to SENASA and MINAE

SENASA stands for "Servicio Nacional de Salud Animal" in Spanish, which translates to the National Animal Health Service in English. SENASA is an institution in Costa Rica responsible for ensuring the health and welfare of animals within the country.

If you see someone mistreating a domestic animal, you can file a report (*denuncia*) with SENASA.

If you see someone mistreating a wild animal, including tour companies that encourage illegal behaviors like feeding or touching wildlife, you can file a report (*denuncia*) online with MINAE's department "SINAC."

NO separation of church and state

Since colonization in the 16th century, Catholicism has played a significant role in shaping the identity of the country, so much so that the Catholic Church is named in the Constitution of Costa Rica.

Yep, you read that correctly. **_NO_** separation of church and state here in Costa Rica. There are only a handful of countries in the world that have a state religion and Costa Rica is one of them.

When the country gained independence in the 19th century, Catholicism was already ingrained in many aspects of society, including its laws and government.

Article 75 of the Constitution of Costa Rica says that, "The Roman Catholic and Apostolic Religion is the religion of the State, which contributes to its maintenance, without preventing the free exercise in the Republic of other forms of worship that are not opposed to universal morality or good practices."

This provision acknowledges Catholicism as the national religion, while ensuring freedom of religion for other beliefs.

However, there are several problems.

The presence of the Catholic Church in the Constitution has influenced public policy for centuries. This results in policies that are influenced by *religious doctrine* rather than being based on secular values and the needs of all citizens.

Rather than evolving with the times, the Constitution's inclusion of the Catholic Church slows down social progress and inclusivity by preserving traditional values that may not align with the beliefs and values of all citizens. Especially now in the 21st century.

Society must evolve with the times... if we don't, progress, for the both the country and its people, will be slowed to a sloth's pace.

The more we know, the more we grow!

How do religion and politics intersect here?

Well, abortion for one.

Illegal. Always. Period.

The Catholic Church's stance against abortion has played a significant role in shaping the country's laws and attitudes toward the issue.

Costa Rica's Penal Code criminalizes abortion except in cases where it is necessary to save the life or physical health of the woman. However, even in these circumstances, there have been significant limitations and legal obstacles.

Do people here want it to be legal?

Public opinion on abortion in Costa Rica is mixed. There are people here that advocate for the legalization, particularly in cases of rape, incest, or when the mother's life is at risk.

On the other end of the spectrum, there are individuals as well as religious and conservative groups, who strongly oppose the legalization of abortion *under any circumstances.*

Do abortions happen here? Yes. Illegally. And not in a safe environment like a doctor's office.

Another intersection is religious education, a mandatory subject taught in public schools (2024).

Equality Prevails

However, even with the Catholic Church being in bed with the government, there have been some changes made here that are noteworthy.

IVF. Legal.

But only since 2015 when the Inter-American Court of Human Rights ordered Costa Rica to lift the ban. Apparently, at the time that it was finally approved in 2015, Costa Rica was the only country in the world to ban IVF! That is how strong the Catholic Church's influence is here.

Nevertheless, it is now permitted, and this landmark decision has allowed couples in Costa Rica to access IVF treatments.

Birth control. Legal.

Plan B / Morning after pill. Legal.

But maybe not for long. It was only approved for general use in 2019. Prior to that, it was illegal unless the woman was sexually assaulted.

One thing that was unclear in my research is that private pharmacies may still have the option to choose whether to dispense it or not. As of 2021, the CCSS has made the medication available for free at the public health clinics.

In March 2024, Catholic bishops in Costa Rica wrote a letter requesting it become illegal again, claiming, "*not everything legal is moral.*"

Same-sex marriage. Legal.

In August 2018, the Supreme Court ruled that the country's ban on same-sex marriage was unconstitutional and discriminatory.

The court gave the legislature 18 months (*from when it was published on November 26, 2018*) to change the law to comply with the ruling.

Following this court decision, the Costa Rican legislature either needed to amend existing laws to allow for same-sex marriage or to leave the court's ruling unaddressed, which would effectively result in the legalization of same-sex marriage *by default* after the 18-month deadline (May 26, 2020).

On May 26, 2020, Costa Rica became the first Central American country to legalize same-sex marriage. However, it seems judges who were appointed before this date have the option to not agree to perform a marriage. Judges appointed after this date do not have that option.

Then, another historical event occurred in June 2020, when it was announced that married same-sex partners would be allowed to adopt.

Times, they are a changing... but it's important to understand that even though these new laws are being enacted, a lot of people here are not in favor. I have seen in groups and heard in person, how expats are bringing their "liberal" mindsets and changing Costa Rica in ways that go against the fundamental beliefs of the country.

It's something to be aware of, that some local people aren't happy about the changes being made.

While many of us view human rights not as "liberal" ideas but as the fundamental right to equal treatment, many people in the world, including people here in Costa Rica, remain closed-minded and resistant to adapting to our modern-day world.

27

Holidays & Observances

Some of these are national holidays, where it is mandatory to have the day off from work (*or paid double time*), whereas others are just recognition days.

New Year's Day (Día de Año Nuevo) - January 1st

Families gather together to share in the spirit of the holiday. At midnight, fireworks light up the sky. In some areas, people may also shoot guns into the sky.

Semana Santa (Easter Week) and Easter Sunday (Domingo de Resurrección) - Date varies, March or April)

"Semana Santa" is the Spanish term for Holy Week, which is the week leading up to Easter Sunday.

While some may say it's a time for reflection and prayer, it seems here in Costa Rica, that contemplative time is all taking place at the beaches. As I live on the coast, I avoid at all costs going out during this week in order to avoid the massive traffic jams around town.

In some places around the country, there are still "dry laws," which means alcohol is not sold on Maundy Thursday and Good Friday.

International Women's Day (Día Internacional de la Mujer) – March 8th

There will sometimes be protests, to bring awareness that Costa Rica still does not provide equal opportunities to its female citizens. This day serves as a reminder of the ongoing struggle for women's rights and the importance of continuing to work towards an inclusive and equitable society.

Juan Santamaría Day (Día de Juan Santamaría) - April 11th

Juan Santamaría Day, celebrated on April 11th, commemorates the heroism and sacrifice of Juan Santamaría, a national hero of Costa Rica. Santamaría is known for his role in the Battle of Rivas on April 11, 1856, during the Filibuster War. The Filibuster War was a conflict between Costa Rica and a group of mercenaries from the US led by William Walker, who aimed to conquer Central American territories.

Santamaría was a poor laborer from Alajuela, who volunteered to set on fire the building where Walker's men were. His courageous act helped turn the tide of the battle in favor of the Costa Rican forces. However, Santamaría was fatally wounded in the process.

Labor Day (Día del Trabajo / Día de la trabajadora/o) - May 1st

Those of you reading this from the United States and Canada might not realize that the majority of the world celebrates Labor Day on May 1st. The day has historical roots in the labor movement and the struggle for workers' rights. However, while the 40-hour work week was an accomplishment of the labor movement, many Tic@s still work a 48-hour work week.

Annexation of the Guanacaste Province (Anexión del Partido de Nicoya) - July 25th

Guanacaste Day, "Dia de la Anexión del Partido de Nicoya," is a national holiday celebrated on July 25th each year. It commemorates the annexation of the province of Guanacaste from Nicaragua in 1824. This is the day when the people in Guanacaste chose to become a part of Costa Rica, a decision made through a democratic vote by its citizens.

Guanacaste Day is celebrated with various cultural events, like parades, traditional dances and music, across the province and the country.

Virgin of Los Ángeles Day (Día de la Virgen de los Ángeles) - August 2nd

August 2nd is celebrated as the Day of the Virgin of Los Ángeles (Día de la Virgen de los Ángeles), a significant religious holiday in Costa Rica.

On this day, thousands of Costa Ricans from all over the country make a pilgrimage to the Basílica de Nuestra Señora de los Ángeles (Basilica of Our Lady of the Angels) in Cartago. Many walk from their homes all around the country as a demonstration of faith, seeking blessings or offering thanks to the Virgin Mary.

The basilica in Cartago houses a small statue of the Virgin Mary, which is believed to have miraculous powers.

Mother's Day (Día de la Madre) - August 15th

Mother's Day, which coincides with the Feast of the Assumption of the Virgin Mary in the Catholic tradition, is celebrated as a national holiday to honor and recognize the significant role of mothers in society.

National Parks Day – August 24th Día de Parques Nacionales de Costa Rica

This day is dedicated to celebrating the country's extensive system of national parks, which are renowned for their biodiversity and wildness. Parks are usually free to the public on this day.

Childrens' Day – September 9th

Known as "Día del(a) Niñ@" in Spanish, Children's Day is observed on September 9th. This day is dedicated to celebrating the importance of children in society, as well as promoting their rights, well-being, and happiness. Schools often hold special assemblies.

Independence Day (Día de la Independencia) - September 15th

Costa Rica's Independence Day marks the country's liberation from Spanish colonial rule in 1821.

Independence Day is commemorated with parades on both the evening of the 14th and the morning of the 15th.

Starting on September 1st, you'll often see flags hanging outside of businesses and homes.

One unique aspect of Costa Rican Independence Day celebrations is the tradition of the "faroles," or lanterns. It signifies the torchbearers that traveled down Central America to announce independence from Spain. The lanterns are made by children using materials such as cardboard and tissue paper, then carried through the streets during the festivities and displayed in homes.

There is also a torch that is carried around the country by different people to commemorate this historic day.

Cultures Day (Día de la Culturas) – October 12th

Hmmm, you may be thinking... Isn't that right around Columbus Day?

Costa Rica did previously observe Columbus Day (Day of the Discovery), much like many other countries in the Americas. He did after all "discover" the country in 1502.

Now, we choose to instead celebrate Día de las Culturas, or Cultures Day. It provides an opportunity to celebrate the diversity that exists here, rather than the colonizers.

But... we do still use the term "colón" for our currency. We haven't completely gotten away from Columbus and the detrimental effects of colonization.

The "colón" is named in honor of Christopher Columbus, who is known as *Cristóbal Colón* in Spanish.

Abolition of the Army – December 1st

December 1st is celebrated as "Día del Abolición del Ejército" or "Army Abolition Day" in Costa Rica. This holiday commemorates the abolition of the country's military forces in 1948.

Christmas Day (La Navidad) - December 25th

Costa Ricans celebrate Christmas with a mix of religious traditions, family gatherings, food, and festive decorations. They usually celebrate Christmas Eve and Midnight Mass. You'll see nativity scenes in front of some homes. There will be fireworks at midnight and some homes will even have Christmas trees (*we do actually have conifers here*).

You can expect fireworks to be shot off every night between Christmas and New Years Day.

As for fireworks on Independence Day, I personally have never experienced that in any town where I've lived. Doesn't mean it doesn't happen, I've just never seen it!

28

Driving, Road Rules & Safety

Driver's License and Requirements

The legal driving age in Costa Rica is 18 years old (2024).

Seatbelt use is mandatory for all passengers. For driving a motorcycle, helmets and reflective gear are required.

Speed limits are posted in kilometers per hour (kph). Because a lot of "highways" are right next to pueblos and there are onramps, schools and homes, speed limits are often no more than 60kph (about 36 mph), and sometimes 80 (about 48mph) in those areas, slowing way down to 25kph (about 15mph) in school zones. Which, for this California girl, is like moving at the pace of an extra tired sloth.

There are times when I find myself going well over the speed limit. It's just what is natural for me when on an open road! But then I catch myself and slow it down...

Contrary to the joke that stop lights are a suggestion here, adhere to traffic lights and road signs diligently.

Don't park next to yellow curbs, fire hydrants or in taxi zones. Your plates can be confiscated, meaning you can't drive the vehicle, and it's a hassle to get them back.

Overtake only when it's safe and legal to do so. Double yellow lines indicate no passing zones.

I've used my hazards here more times in two years of driving than I ever used them in 21 years of driving in California. Defensive driving is an absolute must here!

You'll also need to keep certain things in your car.

Some of these are required by law; others are nice to have...

- Reflective warning triangles
- First aid kit
- Fire extinguisher: Make sure it's rated for vehicles
- Spare tire, jack, and lug wrench

Driving, Road Rules & Safety

- Tire pressure gauge
- Flashlight
- Emergency contact information
- Bottled water and non-perishable snacks

2024 Note: Road rules and regulations change. Please consult updated sources or local authorities for the most up-to-date information.]

How to get your Costa Rica driver's license

Most people who either have a residency application pending or are approved for residency and have their DIMEX will be able to "*homologate*" their driver's license. Which means that you don't need to take the driving test or the written test. As the regulations often change, consider the following as "highlights" and please double check for any new regulations or changes.

You'll need to have your home country's license translated into Spanish and it must be valid/not expired, as well as your passport and DIMEX card (or application paperwork), and a medical exam by a doctor approved to do exams for driving (cost is usually $40-50). You may also need additional proof of your residency. Ask your attorney to help you with that documentation.

Just like with residency, the number of years you get for license renewal appears to be random. I had heard the first renewal should be five years.

When I went to renew, the doctor told me that they were only giving out three-year renewals, and that is what he had just recently received. But when I renewed my license, it had an expiration of five years. The doctor and I were about the same age, so I honestly don't know why he received fewer years!

At this time (2024), you'll need to homologate your license at Cosevi (Costa Rica's DMV), but renewals can be done at BCR (Banco Costa Rica).

To Drive or Not to Drive?

Do you need a car when living in Costa Rica? I mentioned previously that I didn't have a car for the first ten years, so it is indeed possible to live here without one. But as you probably guessed, there are pros and cons to both.

In cities like San José, public transportation options are readily available and can help you get around. However, in more rural areas, having a car can be more convenient. Unless you're way out in the middle of nowhere, there are usually public and private transportation options available.

Getting around, whether it's just to the grocery store or to explore an off-the-beaten-path location, is much easier with your own car. You're also on your own timetable rather than having to wait for a taxi to be available.

While major highways are generally well-maintained, some secondary roads can be rough and challenging, particularly during the rainy season. A 4x4 vehicle may be necessary for certain areas.

Owning a car in Costa Rica can be expensive. You'll need to budget for fuel, insurance, repairs, and annual fees like Marchamo and Dekra.

What is Dekra?

Dekra (formerly called *Riteve*) is an international vehicle inspection company from Germany that conducts vehicle inspections in Costa Rica.

This required service is normally done annually with used cars. It's basically a safety and emissions inspection. There are Dekra stations around the country, including some that "pop up" occasionally in areas where one doesn't exist.

As of 2024, you can get the inspection done one month prior to the month that your sticker expires. *i.e.* Your sticker expires in March, you can make an appointment starting on February 1st. The month of inspection is based on the last digit of your license plate number. For example, a license ending in 8 would be August. The sticker attached to the inside of your windshield also indicates the expiration.

What is Marchamo?

Marchamo is an annual registration permit required by law that allows you to drive the car. It includes mandatory insurance coverage, vehicle registration, and various taxes.

The Marchamo must be renewed each year, and failure to do so can result in fines (*multas*). Marchamo is purchased through INS, the national insurance provider, but some banks also have the option to accept payment for it and give you the sticker.

Marchamo registration opens in November and is due by December 31st. The basic payment has very limited insurance coverage so you will want to speak with them about additional options or talk with a private insurance agent. With INS, you can also purchase additional options, like roadside assistance.

Gas / Diesel

Have you ever noticed there are no signs at gas stations displaying the rates?

That's because the Costa Rica government regulates gas and diesel prices on a nationwide basis. *Meaning...* all gas and diesel prices, no matter what gas station you go to, are the same price.

How to buy a car

Buying a car here involves several steps and considerations. Here's a general guide:

You can buy a car from various sources in Costa Rica, including dealerships, private sellers, or online platforms.

Research the car you want. CRautos.com is a good place to look online, to see what's available and pricing. Local Facebook groups are also a good place to find a vehicle for sale in your area.

Before purchasing a used car, have it inspected by a trusted mechanic. Check the car's condition, mileage, maintenance history, and any signs of damage. Know that it isn't uncommon for an odometer to be "*rolled back.*" There could also be vehicles that were imported and had previously been in wrecks or flooded. Check the VIN whenever possible.

Also ensure the seller of the vehicle is the one who holds the title and there aren't any problems with the title.

Once you agree on a price, you, as the buyer, need to find an attorney. This includes transferring ownership, paying taxes, and obtaining the necessary documentation. In Costa Rica, this is called the *traspaso*.

The buyer normally pays all fees, including attorney's fees.

After completing the transfer of ownership, you'll need to register the vehicle in your name at the National Registry. This involves submitting the necessary paperwork and paying any fees. An attorney will usually do this but be sure it's included in the contract.

Driving, Road Rules & Safety

How not to buy a car (or… my worst mistake made)

Now, let me take you down a dark path into my *worst* mistake made in Costa Rica. With all my medical problems, it became clear that I needed reliable transportation. Relying on taxi's had become challenging. So, when I finally had the opportunity to buy a car, and I found one that I loved, I thought I did everything right.

But I made a lot of mistakes. Here's the short version:

I purchased it from an older local woman and that made me assume she would be trustworthy. Her husband had just passed away and she no longer needed the car. I took it to a mechanic, and everything checked out, even the annual inspection paperwork was clean.

The car had disabled plates as the husband was disabled. But the owner told me: *Don't worry, I can get those changed out in less than two weeks, I have a family member that works for the office that does that.* First mistake. However, in Costa Rica, that is often true – it's all about who you know if you need something done efficiently.

She chose an attorney (second mistake) who, from behind her desk, looked up the car's registration details as she is legally required to do to ensure the title of the car is clean and the sale can proceed.

Well, the attorney told me it was a clean title. (third mistake)

We'll return to that in a second but skipping ahead to my fourth mistake, the seller requested that I pay as much as possible for a deposit. She seemed like a sweet older woman, so I obliged giving her about 90% with 10% still to be paid once the license plates were swapped out.

After I went to the bank, we returned to the attorney's office and the attorney wrote up a contract that explained that with payment of the deposit, the vehicle would be in my possession while we waited for the plates to arrive. Both of us signed the agreement and I drove home in my newly purchased car, as happy as could be.

Then everything fell apart.

As it turned out, the attorney didn't mention to me that the title was held in the dead husband's name and the wife had no legal right to sell it until probate finished. *And there was no way of knowing when probate would be complete. I was told it could take years.*

It was also not disclosed to me that when you sell a vehicle that was originally purchased from an agency with disabled plates, the original owner needs to pay the thousands of dollars of taxes that weren't paid when she originally purchased the vehicle.

That's why the seller needed the money – *in order to pay those taxes.* But this being Costa Rica, paying those taxes isn't a simple matter of making a bank transfer and all is well and good.

NOPE.

To make matters worse, five weeks after the "purchase," I was supposed to move back to the Central Coast, a four-hour drive. Legally, I couldn't drive the vehicle. So, I had to hire a tow truck to take it (*so more money spent towards this purchase*).

The "owner" also couldn't get the license plates quickly... because she had to pay those taxes first and the government agency needed to process all the paperwork.

And once I found out about all of the above, I had to hire my own attorney to manage it all (*as the seller turned out to be both a liar and challenging to deal with in a mature manner*). More money lost.

This story began in the month of October. In January, I received a call from a man associated with a new attorney hired by the seller who threatened me that if I didn't do the transfer that weekend and pay the rest of the money owed, there would be "trouble."

Well, thankfully I didn't transfer the vehicle because as it turned out, the paperwork still wasn't completed for the taxes and had the car been transferred to me, I would have been responsible for those thousands of dollars owed.

It wasn't until May when I finally got the title transferred. The first three attorneys that I tried to hire refused to fight for me. Finally, the fourth attorney I found was able to resolve the situation, after a lot of grief, anxiety and additional money spent. Both on all those attorneys as well as taxis since I couldn't legally drive the car!

None of that was good for the massive health problems that I was having to manage!

Moral of the story: Learn from my mistakes. Don't do what I did.

29

In Case of Emergency

Life in the Jungle Emergency Kit

At one time or another, I needed all of these (*and admittedly, sometimes I didn't have it and it made life so much harder!*).

Some of these items, I have on my Amazon shopping page on my website. Those are the brands I use and recommend (*I may receive a tiny commission if you make a purchase, which helps support me and my small business at no additional cost to you, so thank you!*).

Machete: You'd be surprised how often you may need this.

Duct Tape: Just trust me on this one, it has come in handy.

Flashlight: Power outages happen when you least expect them. Choose a flashlight that can be plugged in and charged when not in use, versus one that has batteries that can wear out.

Candles and a lighter: Just in case the flashlight burns out, have these as a backup!

Super Glue: Repair an item instead of throwing it out! Remember this is a SMALL country. And to once again quote julia butterfly hill, *there is no "away."* Minimize how much trash you throw "away" so that it doesn't become a burden on the country's landfills.

Portable cordless fan with USB charger: If you live in a hot region and the power goes out... just trust me, you'll thank me later. I have a tiny cordless fan (4"x3", *más o menos*) but it is powerful, especially when the power goes out.

Portable power bank: The longest outage I experienced was almost three days. My phone battery died long before then. Fortunately, a kind restaurant owner let me use his outlets to charge my digital devices. But most outages won't last that long, and a power bank will usually suffice until the electricity comes back on.

Surge protector / Battery backup: Not only will it help to protect your devices during power surges, but I have a basic version that I use for my Wi-Fi and when the power went out one time for 8 hours, the Wi-Fi was still working with just the battery backup. I can't plug anything else into it though or it takes up too much energy.

In Case of Emergency

First Aid Kit: Always be prepared!

Multi-Tool / Swiss Army Knife: Everything you need on one little keychain.

Insect Repellent: Keep a bottle in your car for unexpected outings.

Extra water: Always good to have on hand.

How to handle power outages when it's hot

Someone who was building a luxury home once asked in a group – *I'm about to have a baby, and I can't afford solar panels, how can we survive power outages?*

While it may seem his question reeks of entitlement and ignorance, we can use this as a lesson to remember that we all start somewhere... *we don't know what we don't know, until we know it.* Upon moving to Costa Rica, I know I said the wrong thing at times and made lots of mistakes. With a curious mind, we can learn and grow.

My mantra again: Less judgment. More compassion.

Now back to his question. The short answer is... a good majority of locals have homes with metal roofs and no insulation, much less ceiling fans, AC or solar panels, and their babies survive. It is possible to take steps to mitigate the heat during a power outage.

> *A quick note about AC:* If possible, instead of using AC, acclimating is much better for the environment and your wallet!

Okay, with that said, here are some tips for when the power goes out...

Prioritize Safety. Before anything else, ensure the safety of your family, including your pets. If you have children and are concerned, proactively talk with your doctor.

Stay hydrated even if you don't feel thirsty.

Keep your refrigerator and freezer doors closed during power outages to preserve perishable food items for as long as possible.

Wear lightweight, loose-fitting clothing made of breathable fabrics like cotton. You can dampen a cloth with cool water and place it on your forehead or neck, for additional relief.

Limit physical activity. Read a book, play a card game.

If it's safe to leave, go to a place where they do have electricity or somewhere outdoors. The air is always so fresh after a tropical rainstorm!

Embrace a flexible mindset and be prepared to adapt to the challenges posed by outages, whether it's adjusting your daily routine or finding alternative ways to meet your needs.

Stay positive and try not to stress. I know people who freak out every time the power goes out, even if it's only off for five minutes. Remember that outages are _temporary_ inconveniences that can be managed. No need to panic!

PRO TIP: If you know a storm is coming, prep meals early and have on hand easy to make items that don't require electricity.

30

Welcome to the Jungle

Creepy crawlies and other wildlife to be aware of

The following list of wildlife to look out for is not exhaustive. Please always be careful when out in nature.

Snakes

The most venomous and dangerous snake in Costa Rica is the fer-de-lance (*terciopelo*), a type of pit viper. You have very little time to get to a hospital if bitten <u>so do not delay</u>. The venom will not only eat away at your skin, destroying muscle and tissue, it will also kill you if you don't get treatment asap.

Pit vipers, coral and rattlesnakes can all be deadly.

If you find a venomous snake on your property, you can call the local fire department (*bomberos*) and they will come to your home and relocate the

Welcome to the Jungle

snake. They will usually relocate large bee and wasp nests as well.

The coral snake has a rhyme that many people are aware of, but I've been told it doesn't apply to Costa Rica corals: "*Red touch black, safe for Jack. Red touches yellow, kills a fellow*". So if you see something that has similar colors to a coral, contact the fire department for help.

Please do not kill the snake. While it is *very* scary to find one, they are absolutely essential to the ecosystem in this place we get to call home.

Scorpions

Unlike in parts of the US, the sting from a scorpion is usually not lethal here. However, if you're allergic or have any concerns, please seek medical care immediately. An old wives tale that I heard here is to suck on a lime if you get stung and it's supposed to take away the pain.

Army ants

When you first come across these, you might freak out a bit. I've experienced them several times at various homes around the country. There will literally be tens of thousands of them. I am not exaggerating. They will be crawling all over your walls and in your yard. Please don't harm them. They're actually helping you by cleaning up your yard. And trust me, you'll know it when you see them. It is not like a normal path of ants.

Big cats

If you choose to live in a rainforest, friendly reminder that there will be wild animals. It was their home first. Costa Rica has six big cats:

- Jaguar
- Puma
- Ocelot
- Margay
- Oncilla
- Jaguarundi

The good news is that you'll likely never see a jaguar and while pumas are often seen in places like Corcovado, they are less likely to attack (it has happened though, so do be aware). Coming from California, mountain lions (*pumas*) attack humans there. Here's why:

California has destroyed their natural habitat. While Costa Rica is unfortunately on its way to overdeveloping its land, for now, there have been very few reported cases of a big cat approaching or harming a human.

They have enough space and food to survive without taking on another animal (*us, the human species)* that is larger than them. Big cats also tend to be nocturnal and in general, I don't recommend walking around the jungle at night... But do always be careful and prepared for anything you might come across.

Crocodiles

Many people believe crocodiles are only at Tarcoles. I actually just saw a tourist tell this to a concerned traveler in a Facebook group. When I say there is A TON of misinformation in Facebook groups, I really do mean it.

Saying they only exist in Tarcoles is far from true. Crocodiles can be found throughout the country, at river mouths, in the ocean and inland.

There was even a crocodile found at the Quepos public hospital, hanging out in the *inside* garden area. Yes... *inside* the doors of the hospital.

And a few other creatures that you don't want to touch:

- Brazilian wandering spider
- Caterpillars
- Bullet ants
- Fire ants
- Jellyfish
- Stingrays
- Tarantulas

- Wasps and bees *(we do have a stingless bee, but I still wouldn't recommend touching it)*
- Poison dart frogs

A few tips if you live in a jungle setting:

Don't leave food out in the open as it can attract animals. Elevate your trash receptacle and only put trash out on the day it's picked up.

Maintain your yard, keep grass cut short. Don't walk through tall grass without rubber boots, or even snake gaiters for extra precaution. Avoid piles of leaves or wood where scorpions, snakes and other creatures like to hang out.

Invest in snake tongs if you feel comfortable handling a snake yourself. I would still recommend calling the fire department.

Cut away any *branches* that are near your roofline. *Please don't cut down the tree!*

Educate yourself about the types of animals in your area and their behaviors.

Remember this is their home, too. Please minimize the damage you cause to their environment. Chose to create a safe haven for all, *you and them.*

31

Shopping

Other than groceries, I personally don't feel the need to do much shopping here. A simple lifestyle with morning sun, an afternoon storm, a huge collection of books, my garden and my two adopted cats are generally all that I need.

And for the time being, I don't live near the city so there aren't many stores where I could go shopping anyways.

But for those of you who do love to shop, the big malls in San José will have all the stores you could possibly want, but usually at a much higher price point than what you're used to. To see a list of all the stores in one of the popular malls, google "*Multiplaza Escazu.*"

Be mindful of fake brands (especially with shoes). That is a rampant problem here, with very little quality control.

Now let's talk about food!

Food is always a basic need so in this section we'll take a look at the types of grocery stores and what you can expect...

First off, depending on where you live and how picky you are, you may need to go to more than one "*super*" to get your food for the week. Currently, I live on the Central Coast and even with all the arrivals of new products that have happened over the years, I still go to at least two, if not three, grocery stores each week.

Sometimes one place carries a brand that I like, and the other place doesn't carry that product at all. But the other store will have the spinach that I like, and another place will have the kale that I like.

One place has the amazing sourdough bread that I have never found anywhere else. Well, technically there are two other local places that have sourdough, but they taste more like French bread in a sourdough shape.

You get the picture... if you like certain products, you may have to bounce around a bit to different stores.

The pulpería is the most basic and smallest type of grocery store. It's like a mini 7-11. It will have beans and rice, gum, sodas and junk food. As far as fresh veggies and fruits are concerned, that can sometimes be a hit or miss situation. Oftentimes they seem to be not so fresh, more like they're usually on their way out. It's one of those places where you just grab a few items.

The second type of grocery store is the mid-level *super*. I would say Pali and Maxi Pali (*both owned by Walmart*) would fall into this category as well as anything that calls itself a *Super*. In these stores, you'll find more options than at the pulpería.

A friend once told me that they went into Pali looking for peanut butter and couldn't find it. So, they may not have everything that you want but they will have more options for you to choose from.

The third type of grocery store are the bigger stores like Walmart and Pricesmart. Pricesmart is just like Costco. You're going to walk in and think that you're back in the US. They even have some of the same products, *but they are not owned by Costco.*

Pricesmart reminds me of going to Price Club in the 90's… sometimes they have a product, and the next time, they're out of stock.

Walmart will have more items than a mid-level super, but still some imported items will be difficult to find.

The fourth type of supermarket is the higher end type of store that carries highly taxed, very expensive, imported products. BM and Compre Bien are examples.

They may not carry everything you want, but they do have more of the types of things that expats are looking for.

AutoMercado falls into this category as well, it's a larger grocery store and very expensive. I call it the Whole Foods of Costa Rica.

The most important type of grocery store? The *feria*. I know, not technically a grocery store.

Going every week to your farmers market, you get to meet and talk with the local growers and see what's in season. You get to see what they're growing, and taste new foods that maybe you've never tried before.

Also at farmers markets, you can connect with local artisans who are selling what they make. It's a beautiful way to connect with your community and to support the local people.

If you can't get to a farmers' market, the next best choice is a *verdulería*: a fruit and veggie store or a roadside stand.

Shopping

> PRO TIP – Check for expired products before purchasing. Unlike in some countries where expired products are promptly removed from shelves, here, it's not uncommon to find them lingering. Look for "*vence*" and the date.

Good to know Spanish words for the grocery store

- ¿Dónde está...? - Where is...?
- ¿Cuánto cuesta? - How much does it cost?
- ¿Tiene...? - Do you have...?
- El carrito - The shopping cart
- Pan - Bread
- Frutas - Fruits
- Verduras - Vegetables
- Arroz - Rice
- Frijoles - Beans
- Aceite - Oil
- Sal - Salt
- Azúcar - Sugar
- Sin gluten - Gluten-free
- Sin lactosa - Lactose-free
- Efectivo - Cash
- Recibo - Receipt
- Oferta - Offer
- Descuento - Discount
- Abierto - Open
- Cerrado - Closed

32

Shipping

Shipping within the country

Correos is the "postal service" for Costa Rica. I wouldn't recommend it for shipping outside the country (*except for postcards*) but it is generally reliable – and reasonably priced – for shipping within the country. They even give tracking numbers! Many locations also have PO boxes.

Encomienda is another option. While historically the word referred to a system of slave labor during the Spanish colonization, now, *encomienda* refers to a courier service where individuals or businesses can send packages to others around the country. Sometimes the item will be sent on a bus and you'll pick it up at a bus station and sometimes it's sent by courier.

> PRO TIP: Whether shipping in country or international, be sure to include your local phone number so that the delivery company can contact you, if they aren't sure of where you live.

Shipping

How to get packages from abroad

Wondering how you can get packages delivered to you in Costa Rica from outside the country?

First, let's address the "address" question. You do indeed have an address, even if it's not anything like you're used to. If renting, ask your property owner and if you own, you should have received either an address or a "description."

To receive packages, there are a few options:

1. Join a Facebook group here people ask for help bringing items into the country. Be wary however as some people have reported problems with this method.

2. Order from Amazon and have them ship direct to your home in Costa Rica. There are limitations, *not everything can be shipped here*, and it's costly. But usually, Amazon takes care of all customs taxes and shipping costs. Average speed of delivery is around 7-14 days.

If you live way out in the middle of nowhere, delivery services may be limited, so you might have to drive to a nearby town to pick up what you've ordered.

3. Order from anywhere and have it shipped to a freight forwarder in Miami. The cost is usually per pound or kilo plus applicable taxes.

There are still some limitations on what can be shipped, talk with the shipper about what is permitted to send and what is not allowed. Some will help you get products like supplements and cat food, while others will not.

Also be aware – there are some that provide excellent customer service and others, not so much.

4. Another option is a service like Borderfree.com which also has the option to include both shipping and customs taxes and will usually deliver to your door.

But it can be more expensive. Not just the shipping and customs taxes but also the prices of the items.

Several years ago, I compared prices in US dollars on Macy's international website to their US website. The prices on the international site were higher even though the currency was the same.

5. "Mule" it in. Send friends a large duffel or plastic bin and ask them to please help you out with bringing items into the country. Then ship

Shipping

all the items you need to them and have them bring it as one of their pieces of luggage.

WARNING! Well-meaning friends and family may want to send you care packages. Have them shipped to a freight forwarder in Miami. And still confirm what they're putting inside the box as not everything may be allowed.

Shipping direct to Costa Rica will, more often than not, land your packages in customs jail and, depending on what was sent, you may or may not be able to get them out.

It could also cost you a pretty penny, not to mention the time and energy to have to go to the customs agency (often Puntarenas or San José) or find a customs broker.

33

The Dark Side of Paradise

As an outsider looking in, Costa Rica may seem to be a picture-perfect paradise. But scratch below the surface *and just like other places all around the world,* you'll find a darker reality that many are hesitant to acknowledge or discuss.

But we will never grow and progress as a country if we continue to sweep all the bad stuff under the rug. While I may not have a right to vote, this is the country I call home and I do want to see its people prosper.

In this chapter, I'm not painting the country or its people with a single brushstroke, but rather my intention is to shed light on some of the historical and present-day challenges that exist.

Why I think sharing the dark side is absolutely necessary:

By openly discussing the dark side of paradise, we raise awareness, disrupt the status quo and challenge existing power structures... so that we can become a part of the solution, rather than the problem.

Just because we can't fix everything, doesn't mean we shouldn't do something. Every action counts.

When we commit ourselves to the betterment of those around us and become active participants in this place we call *home*, we not only find a deeper sense of belonging but also help shape the kind of world we want to live in.

To begin, here's a *snapshot* of why people shy away from discussing the dark side of paradise:

Human beings are inherently drawn to what's "good," doing so offers solace and hope. Discussions that are about downsides and difficulties threaten to shatter these illusions, making individuals confront uncomfortable truths that may challenge their beliefs and perceptions.

READ THIS SECTION ANYWAYS!

Also, people with investments in the country might be afraid of damaging the country's reputation, which could potentially affect their financial interests.

Not acknowledging the dark side also sets up many expats for failure. If you arrive with rose-colored glasses on, it can be a lot more difficult to accept the reality upon arrival.

You might not like everything you read in this chapter. Please have a curious mind and remember, *no country is perfect*. As you read through each section, think about what YOU can do differently. Each of us can make a positive difference.

Shall we begin?

Examples of the downsides include:

- Economic disparities
- Tourism-driven inequality
- Gentrification
- Poverty
- Deforestation and habitat loss
- Pollution and pesticides
- Violent crime
- Organized crime and drug trafficking
- Public healthcare system
- Ethnic and racial discrimination
- Gender inequality

How not to be taken advantage of

It's true that the people of Costa Rica are very friendly and helpful. But remember what I said in the beginning about "all or none" type situations? *This is again one of those...*

Time and again, I've heard stories of expats being taken advantage of, not just by locals but by foreigners as well. "Being gringoed" is the term that is often used. And it should be noted, locals get taken advantage of too.

Some people I know have lost tens of thousands of dollars to either businesses that they thought were reputable or individuals who they thought they could trust.

I had one attorney (*who was Tica*), tell me: TRUST NO ONE. She even said she doesn't trust her family! That's an extreme example but there are a lot of people in this world who aren't reliable or honest and unfortunately stories of that happening here on the Rich Coast are abundant.

Besides resilience and a realistic mindset, due diligence and discernment are two of the most important traits to have in your mental toolbox when you're living in Costa Rica.

For some of us, the idea of being scammed or taken advantage of is hard to get our head wrapped around. Especially when everyone seems so friendly! I know that in my 37 years living in California, while life wasn't perfect, I had never been scammed.

So, if this isn't the sort of thing you're used to, it might feel strange living life on the defensive... but I strongly recommend it.

> NB: Being on the defensive doesn't mean you need to live in fear or be constantly anxious, but rather, just become more aware.

Here's a few ways to avoid being scammed:

- Seek advice from professionals
- Carefully review all contracts
- Be wary of attorneys, they don't always give the best, or accurate, advice.
- Remember, just because someone comes across as a nice person, doesn't mean you can trust them. Ask for referrals.

Types of scams include fraudulent real estate deals, fake bank calls or calls from the hospital saying they need your bank account info.

ATM scams: Skimmers and hidden cameras can be used to steal card information at ATMs. Choose ATMs located in well-lit, secure areas.

Taxi scams: Some taxi drivers might take advantage by taking longer routes or not using the meter (called the *Maria* here), resulting in higher fares. It's advisable to use official taxis and ensure the meter is running.

Police bribes: This has only happened to me in Nicaragua (*and I'm not even sure they were really police*). However, I've heard of it repeatedly happening here in Costa Rica so it's worth mentioning. It is illegal and I don't recommend paying them off as it only continues the corruption and abuse of power. But if you feel unsafe, do what you need to do to protect yourself.

Overcharging: Prices for goods and services might be inflated. Always ask for prices upfront and get multiple bids in order to compare.

A representative from the bank calls you and needs permission for one thing or another. They tell you they need access to your account. HANG UP IMMEDIATELY.

Payment is requested for delivery of something you've purchased, before receiving it. CASH ON DELIVERY **ONLY**. I can't stress that one enough.

Construction scams. People pay a large percentage up front to "help cover costs". Even if the contractor says they can get materials at a discount (*and you verify that with your own cost comparison*), pay for the materials yourself, directly with the hardware store, and create a schedule to pay the contractor as they progress.

DON'T PAY UP FRONT. Even if it's only 5-10%. Once again... **Cash on delivery.**

And let's look at the many types of gas station scams:

Shortchanging: Ensure that the pump resets to zero before refueling.

Credit Card Skimming: I've heard of this one happening repeatedly but I'm not sure how it's done. I imagine a skimming device is placed on the credit card reader to steal credit card information from unsuspecting customers.

Unauthorized Charges: Check your credit card or bank statements regularly for any unauthorized charges after refueling.

Fake Gasoline: In rare cases, there have been reports of gas stations selling diluted gasoline, which can damage your vehicle's engine. Stick to well-known and reputable gas stations to minimize the risk of purchasing watered-down gasoline.

If something feels too good to be true or if you feel uncomfortable in a situation, trust your instincts and proceed with caution. It's better to be safe than sorry.

Fun fact... research is being done on "gut feelings" and evidence is showing that our intuition is indeed real. So, learning how to tap into that "gut" sense can go a long way in protecting yourself from scams here on the Rich Coast.

Corruption

In Costa Rica, corruption scandals have involved kickbacks, bribery, and other forms of illegal activity in government contracts, including a big one in recent years related to road construction, leading to delays, cost overruns, and sometimes the incomplete construction of infrastructure projects or use of inferior materials, compromising quality and safety.

President Rodrigo Chaves Robles, who took office in May 2022, has taken steps to address these issues and strengthen its legal and institutional framework to combat corruption.

But let me say this loud and clear: **Corruption still very much exists here.**

Crime

People may want to deny it, but if you watch the news, and join a few crime groups, you'll see that crime exists here and is a problem.

Many will downplay it by saying, *it's just the gangs and drug dealers.* While that is a big part of the crime here, it's not the only type of crime.

They may also say, ...*all other types of crime are "petty."*

I have personally known people here who were held up at gunpoint (*locals and foreigners*) or knifepoint (*myself included*), taken hostage in their homes and beaten, kidnapped and even murdered. I can't say the same for my 37 years of living in California.

Regarding the gangs and drug dealers, it's important to note that they don't just fight in the middle of the night in a back alley.

Innocent people have been caught in the crossfire *during the day* and injured or killed. These types of incidents happen in public, with regular people around, including children.

And while some expats might come from a place where this is only common in an "inner city," it's happening here in places like Tamarindo and Quepos.

Also to be aware of, the justice system here is severely inadequate. Most criminals aren't caught or if they are, they aren't sent to prison or spend very little time in one. They also don't come out rehabilitated.

> **Empathy note:** If someone tells you they've been robbed, avoid responding by saying you've never been robbed, as it can imply victim blaming or suggest that you're more cautious or superior. Also, refrain from dismissing their experience with "*it happens everywhere*," which can diminish the seriousness of what they've gone through.

Abuse

While again, the general consensus is *"everyone is friendly"* here, the reality is that abuse happens, just like everywhere else in the world. To both locals and foreigners.

Domestic Violence: Reports of domestic and dating violence have increased dramatically in recent years. This includes physical, sexual, psychological, and financial abuse. This increase could also be because more women are feeling empowered (*hopefully*) to report it now.

Child Abuse: Child abuse, including physical, sexual, and emotional abuse, is also a problem. The National Child Welfare Agency (PANI) handles child abuse cases and offers assistance to victims, yet challenges such as underreporting and a lack of adequate resources for prevention and intervention persist.

Sexual Violence: As of 2023, Costa Rica is #7 country in the world for having the highest *reported* rates of rape.

Very sad fact:

Research has shown that 911 calls for violence against women increases during football games (*soccer for those of you from the US).*

At one point, one of the local teams added a third scoreboard for all the 911 calls received during the game that were for "violence against women."

While that kind of awareness is imperative in creating change, unfortunately, they have found that the majority of the calls for violence against women actually happen in the hours and days after the game.

Let's remember that a lot of abuse and sexual violence also goes unreported.

Hate speech

A recent United Nations study researched the overwhelming amount of hate speech here. Conducted over two years, here's how it was broken down, from the most to the least.

- Politics
- Sexual Orientation
- Gender
- Xenophobia
- Generational Clash
- Religion
- Racism
- Disability

Indigenous People

Colonization by the Spanish in the 16th century led to the displacement and death of many Indigenous communities, as well as imposing foreign customs, languages, and systems of governance on the original residents.

Just like in other parts of the world, this legacy of colonialism has had enduring effects involving land rights as well as social and economic challenges and ongoing discrimination and stigmatization.

There are eight communities here: Maleku, Cabécar, Bribri, Chorotega, Bröran, Ngäbe, Huetar, and Brunka.

In recent years, two Indigenous leaders were murdered by people outside their communities.

In 2019, Sergio Rojas Ortiz (59), a leader for the Bribri people, was assassinated by 15 bullets entering his body for trying to protect his Indigenous land. The case was dismissed in 2024. However, justice may still be served by the Inter-American Commission on Human Rights.

In 2020, Yehry Rivera (45), from the Brörán people, was shot and killed by a Tico farmer. The farmer was apparently celebrated by his community for the murder. That celebration was used as evidence, and he was sentenced to 22 years in prison.

There is legislation from 1977 that grants land ownership to Indigenous tribes (approximately 7% of the country's land); however, the law has never been implemented. Nearly 50 years later, only two of the twenty-four territories have been fully returned to the Indigenous communities.

A Special Rapporteur from the UN visited in 2021 to discuss the ongoing land law disputes and reported his concern about, *"the structural racism that pervades the judiciary, especially at the local level, the lack of effective measures to protect human rights defenders and the impunity for crimes committed against land defenders."*

More Sad Facts: Less than 2% of today's population in Costa Rica are Indigenous people.

They were only given the right to vote in 1994. 30 years ago, from the time of the first printing of this book.

Racism

Racism does indeed exist here, albeit often subtly and deeply ingrained within societal structures.

Like other countries, Costa Rica has a historical legacy of slavery. While slavery was officially abolished in 1824 (*41 years before the US*), stereotypes and discrimination exist today.

Additionally, *colorism*, or the preference for lighter skin tones, is prevalent in Costa Rica, reflecting broader societal attitudes towards race. Lighter-skinned individuals often have more privileges and opportunities denied to their darker-skinned counterparts. (*Here again, remember, this is <u>not</u> an always or never situation.*)

Xenophobia, hatred expressed towards people from other countries, also can rear its ugly head. A statement I've heard many times here, whenever something bad has happened is... *Well, it must have been the Nicaraguans. Or the Panamanians.* And lately, *the Venezuelans.*

If you're from the US, you may have heard something similar... *Well, it must have been the Mexicans.* Even though there is often no proof. It's simply an easy way to blame someone else and maintain a superior "us versus them" mentality, while not taking responsibility for the problems that exist in the country.

There has also been unjustified hate speech expressed towards other nationalities outside of the Americas. Much of this comes from the kind of Nationalism that exists here, which we'll review shortly.

Pet crisis

There is an overwhelming population of both abused and abandoned cats and dogs in Costa Rica.

I belong to a lot of different community groups around the country and the amount of animal abuse that I see is disheartening and discouraging. My heart breaks every time I see yet another story of animal abuse and abandonment.

Spaying and neutering programs exist, mostly from nonprofit organizations, and they are usually at a very low cost. However, cultural attitudes towards pet guardianship contribute to the problem.

Around the country, many pets are not regarded as cherished members of the family. This mentality results in either abuse or abandonment, when pets become inconvenient or burdensome to their guardians.

There is also a mentality of machismo when it comes to castration (*yes, for real, some Tic@s have told me this is an underlying reason why they won't neuter male dogs*).

Animal shelters and rescue organizations in Costa Rica are often overwhelmed by the sheer number of homeless animals. Limited resources (*human, financial and physical space*) mean that many strays go without proper care and attention, exacerbating their suffering.

How can you help alleviate the plight of the stray population, creating a safer and more humane environment for all?

You can become a volunteer at a local animal shelter, or become a foster pet parent.

And please, PLEASE, **_PLEASE,_** if you adopt a pet, make sure you're giving it a forever home. Even if you move back to your home country, or get pregnant or for any other reason, accept the responsibility that you are now their guardian for life. If you can't make that commitment, then perhaps a better option would be to simply foster pets and help them get placed into homes. Choose to be a part of the solution.

Pesticide Use

While Costa Rica is often seen as THE place for green living, once again, when we look beneath the surface, the reality tells a different story: *Costa Rica is among the world's top consumers of pesticides per capita.*

And up until 2017, it was the #1 user of pesticides and herbicides... IN THE WORLD.

Yep, for real.

This often-overlooked fact not only poses significant environmental threats but also carries serious health implications for those of us living here.

The Dark Side of Paradise

The reality is we have A LOT of bugs, fungi, and out of control weeds here. And using chemicals is an easy and fast way to eradicate them.

However, this heavy reliance on pesticides has led to a range of concerning issues. And while this section may make me sound like an alarmist, I feel it's imperative to bring it to light so that you can become aware and make your own informed decision on the matter.

The rampant use of pesticides has taken a severe toll on the country's biodiversity. Spraying of chemical compounds has resulted in the contamination of soil, waterways, and ecosystems, endangering countless species of flora and fauna.

The indiscriminate use of pesticides has contributed to the decline of pollinators like bees and butterflies, vital for the pollination of crops and the maintenance of ecological balance.

> *Bees are considered endangered here and estimates suggest they may become extinct by 2035... which would be a gigantic problem for humans, food security and our precious planet.*

Beyond its environmental impact, the excessive use of pesticides in Costa Rica has dire consequences for public health. Exposure to toxic chemicals has been connected to various health issues, including respiratory problems, neurological disorders, reproductive issues, and certain types of cancer.

It's not just the agricultural workers who are at risk. We, the consumers, are at risk as well. Costa Rica has a high amount of cancer at a rate of approximately 175-200 cases for every 100,000 people, with the highest types being prostate, breast, and colorectal. The survival rate is less than half.

While some research will tell you the two aren't related, do you really want to take the chance with your health and the health of your family?

Wash your fruits and veggies thoroughly and remember that the animals you eat are eating the grass, hay and grains that are also being sprayed. And don't get me started on the fish in the ocean and all the toxins found in their bodies.

Remember too, DDT has only been banned here since 1998 and it likes to hang around for a while in both the soil and water (*read Rachel Carson's Silent Spring if you're interested in learning more*).

There are some 3rd party "certifiers" for organic food, but their standards may differ from those you're accustomed to, in your home country.

Do your due diligence and always thoroughly wash your fruits and veggies, even if the seller claims it's organic.

Deforestation

Between the 1950's and the 1980's, it's estimated that between 60-80% of the country's forests were clearcut for cows and other agriculture. Millions of acres of trees were cut down. At one point, over 125,000 acres of land were clearcut *annually*. During that time, Costa Rica had the highest rate of deforestation in all of Latin America.

Not only is that harmful for the air we breathe, but just take a moment to think of all the other plant life that died, as well as the wildlife that was displaced and likely died because they lost their homes.

In the mid-90's, new laws were enacted to protect, preserve and reforest *some* of the land. But forest regeneration can take hundreds of years, and that's only if we start taking care of the land now. Unfortunately, some of the reforested land has already been clear-cut *again*.

Climate change isn't making things any easier. Scientists say that regeneration projects might not work here because of the increased temperatures. It's just too hot in some areas for the forests to recover and thrive.

And let's remember, there are roughly one billion cows in the world, and they also contribute to those increased temperatures. We don't need that many cows, nor would there be that many cows if humans didn't eat them. But they are artificially inseminated in order to keep up with the demands for beef and dairy.

Some may see this story of Costa Rica's shift away from massive deforestation as a transformation. But it is also a warning.

Today, forests in Costa Rica continue to be cut down and areas that could be reforested remain dry landscapes with grassy pastures to feed the cows that will be slaughtered and sold as beef, locally and internationally.

I urge you to be a part of the solution. I'm not saying you have to stop eating animals. But please consider your daily choices and the ripple effects they have, not only on your life but for future generations as well.

> *"Only when the last tree has died, the last river has been poisoned, the last fish has been caught— will we realize we cannot eat money."*
> – Indigenous Proverb

Gentrification

The old neighborhood gets an upgrade... while some may say *"woohoo!,"* others are feeling left out.

Why, you may ask?

It's not all sunshine and rainbows because along with the upgrades often come higher living expenses and a community atmosphere that's less like the old pueblo.

One of the reasons I left Tamarindo was because it felt like there were only a handful of Tic@s who could actually afford to live in the town. *In my opinion,* it felt like a beach town in the US. And I moved to Costa Rica to get out of the US!

Gentrification is a classic tale of two sides to the same coin. On one hand, it brings investment and revitalization. But on the flip side, it can also lead to displacement, inequality, and the loss of community identity.

I first wrote about gentrification in Costa Rica over ten years ago. While it is being discussed more now, this is not a new problem.

So how do we find the balance between progress and preservation?

For many who have called these communities home for generations, the changes can bring both opportunities and challenges.

The surge in tourism and development can lead to the creation of job opportunities, providing locals with a source of income to support their families.

Improved infrastructure and amenities can enhance the quality of life for residents, with better access to services such as healthcare, education, and transportation.

But that is only if they can afford those added amenities. More often than not, those new amenities cater more to foreigners than to the local population.

As demand for property increases, so do housing prices, making it increasingly difficult for locals to afford to live in their own towns.

These "local" communities may begin to collapse as they become increasingly commercialized to cater to tourists and expats. For example, Marina Pez Vela in Quepos shoots off fireworks on July 4th. That is *not* Costa Rica's Independence Day.

Locals who decide to stay might experience feelings of bitterness as they see their once-recognizable neighborhoods turn into playgrounds for wealthy newcomers.

It's really a double-edged sword for locals. While it may bring economic opportunities and modern amenities, it also threatens to displace and disenfranchise those who have called these communities home for generations.

What can you do about it?

Take time to see what's happening in your community. See how you can help support and lift up the locals who may be feeling displaced. Choose to frequent locally owned businesses who you know to be good business owners, taking care of their employees.

Choose a home that has a smaller footprint. You probably don't need a 1,500+ sq ft home, much less 3,000 or 5,000.

If you *really* want to integrate and "live like a local" (as many expats proclaim is their intention), then you should be aware that most Tic@ homes are generally **under 1,000 sq ft in size**. And that's including anything exterior, under the roofline! And yes, multiple people *can and do* live in these smaller homes. They often don't have luxury amenities. Some still have dirt floors. They also tend to be *very* eco-friendly.

Will you swap out your:

- ✓ Dishwasher for a drying rack?
- ✓ Dryer for a clothesline?
- ✓ Bathtub for a shower?
- ✓ Air-conditioning for a ceiling fan or a floor fan?
- ✓ Hot water for cold, or a "suicide" shower?

Prioritizing smaller-scale, energy-efficient homes can minimize both the environmental footprint as well as the demand for "McMansions" that often drive gentrification.

Nationalism

Costa Ricans (*not all, but some*) have a high degree of Nationalism. And you may be thinking, *Hey, that's great, they're proud of their country!*

I've said this before: Nationalism fuels intolerance.

Whether you're religious or not, remember there is a reason why *pride* is one of the seven deadly sins. Let's take a look at a few of the downsides of Nationalism, and not just here but in any country (*because it exists everywhere*)...

Nationalism can foster an "us vs. them" mentality, towards people who they consider outsiders or different. This can result in discrimination and social tensions. It may discourage openness to new ideas, influences, and perspectives from outsiders.

Nationalism emphasizes holding onto the "old ways" at all costs, rather than acknowledging the changing times and encouraging inclusivity and harmony.

It can also promote a distorted view of history, glorifying certain events or people while downplaying or ignoring others.

I've heard locals assert: *We have no problems here.* And they seem to really believe that. Nationalism creates blind spots. Problems that require attention and resolution can be minimized or ignored entirely. Progress stops when we choose not to address the elephant in the room.

If you asked me, "*Chrissy, wouldn't you be upset if someone was putting down the US?*"

My answer would be *No...* because while the US has many positive qualities, I can admit that there are a whole lot of problems and I'd rather address them than sweep them under the rug, pretending like they don't exist.

What if there was another way to be a good citizen, without all the downsides?

Let me introduce you to one of my favorite but all too often unused and unknown terms: *Cosmopolitanism*. Or as I like to call it, a citizen of the earth.

This was one of my most important takeaways from graduate school as it had a profound impact on how I see the world and how I choose to show up.

Cosmopolitanism originated with the Stoics and shares with us a vision of inclusivity and interconnectedness (*two of my favorite words*), wherever we live in the world. Because if you look at our planet from space, you'll realize there really are no borders.

It encourages us to move beyond parochialism ethnocentrism, and I would add even anthropocentrism, to embrace the rich mosaic of human cultures, languages, and traditions that make up our global community *as well as valuing everything that exists on this planet we get to call home, not just the humans.*

Practicing cosmopolitanism in our everyday lives involves adopting a mindset of openness, curiosity, and humility towards the world around us.

It means stepping outside of our comfort zones to interact with individuals from diverse backgrounds and viewpoints.

It invites us to share a more inclusive vision of humanity so that we can create a world that is more compassionate, tolerant, and connected, where every individual is valued and respected for who they are.

How does cosmopolitanism differ from nationalism?

While nationalism is *exclusive* in nature, cosmopolitanism invites you to be a part of an *inclusive* community. Where everyone is welcome.

It's like expanding your social circle to include friends from all around the globe, each bringing their own unique contributions.

Instead of building walls, we'd rather build bridges – connecting with others, sharing experiences, and finding common ground.

Nationalism has its place, *for sure* – it's important to honor where you come from and the values you hold dear. But cosmopolitanism adds a little extra sparkle to the mix. It's like opening the windows wide to see the world as a vibrant mosaic, not just a monotonous monoculture.

Make easy hard

There's a gif in WhatsApp of a brunette girl with a ponytail who is banging her head against a concrete wall. That is often (*for me*) what "make easy hard" feels like.

It's been a while since I wrote this so... *friendly reminder, things are different here.*

In a country where you'd think simplicity would prevail, it often seems like every "to-do" is needlessly complicated, turning the most basic of tasks into overwhelming challenges.

Once again, I'm going to ask you to scratch beneath the surface, and you'll find a system where simplicity often turns into complexity at the hands of bureaucracy, red tape and inefficiency.

From waiting for approval of your pending residency application to dealing with the healthcare system, every endeavor is often met with unnecessary obstacles. Even mundane tasks like renewing a driver's license or paying taxes can become nightmares of frustration and wasted time.

There was a second time that I tried to get records from the public health system. In order to get the records, I had to pay a few colones to a man outside the hospital, in a makeshift tarp structure, to get a "timbre" (stamp). Then I took that stamp inside and gave it to the woman behind the desk. Two weeks later, I was able to pick up the records (*and of course they weren't what I had actually needed*).

I can appreciate that this is a way for that gentlemen under the tarp outside the hospital to earn a little extra cash. But it still seems cumbersome and unnecessary.

Another less-than-ideal story, my residency application took six years to get approved. It was one problem after another. It shouldn't have been that hard or taken that long. Patience truly is a virtue here in Costa Rica.

But what's most frustrating for me is how inefficiency often makes life so much harder for the local people.

I realize it's what's "normal" and they're used to it. But spending hours standing in a long line as the sun rises in the hopes of getting a doctor's appointment that day seems so wasteful and a way of keeping the citizens from progressing and ever getting ahead. And if they aren't chosen, they have to return the next day and try again.

Or being elderly and having to drive three hours to San José to have an MRI at 10pm at the public hospital and then drive back home in the middle of the night because spending the money on a hotel wasn't possible. Not only inefficient but dangerous.

I recently had a virtual appointment with a private specialist. As we talked, he realized I needed to see another specialist and he told me that since he works both privately and for the public hospital, he could write me a referral to a specialist at the public health system.

I thought to myself, "*great!*" Since another doctor at the EBAIS was supposed to do the same referral two years before and never did, this was an improvement.

But (*there always seems to be a but*), I'd have to pick up the referral from his office which was over an hour from my house. I can't drive long distances anymore, so I had to hire a driver.

Then on another day, I had to hire a driver to take me two hours to a different part of the country, to drop the paper off at the specialist's office inside a public hospital.

I dropped off the paper and was told I'd eventually see an appointment date in the EDUS app.

The point of this story is: getting a referral *should* be a simple process of entering the information into a computer system that is connected nationwide to all public hospitals. Or picking up the phone and speaking to someone. Or sending an email!

Efficiency can create opportunities. Doing the same thing again and again because *that's how it's always been done...* well, that's a loose definition of insanity. AND it prevents progress and growth for the people of the country.

But all hope is not lost. There are signs of change on the horizon. Shifts are slowly happening to modernize and streamline the country's institutions. And thankfully, more and more, the government is introducing technology to simplify processes and reduce the nightmare of bureaucratic bottlenecks.

34

Be a Good Expat

In this chapter are some of the *faux pax's* that I've seen (*and some mistakes that I've personally made*) since moving to Costa Rica.

I'm not suggesting that you would personally engage in any of these behaviors, rather my intention is to highlight a few topics that might not be common knowledge to everyone. So, consider this an effort to shed some light on these issues.

FAQ: Can I work in Costa Rica?

I believe strongly in integrity and authenticity, so I'll share here that when I first arrived, there were no expat FB groups that I was aware of, and very little information in order to learn the do's and don'ts.

The learning curve was high, and I made a few mistakes along the way. I started a business, but I didn't hire Tic@s until a few months after arriving. I was also asked by a local hotel to teach yoga and I was happy to do so.

But then I learned...

Don't take jobs away from Tic@s. It's not just a moral issue but also a legal one.

Unless you have a *very* specialized skill that a local can't do, you are not legally allowed to work in the country until you have permanent residency. There are workarounds but again I'll repeat: *Do you really want to take a job away from a local?*

You can, however, start a business here. You're still not legally allowed to work in the business until you have permanent residency, but you can train and hire locals. Remember the old adage: *give more than you receive.*

And to get out ahead of this one as it is often proclaimed, *"But everyone else is doing it!"*

Just because everyone else is doing it, doesn't mean you should.

How to Avoid a Sense of Entitlement When Moving to Costa Rica

Some expats arrive in Costa Rica with a sense of entitlement versus humility and respect. Many might not even realize that they're doing it.

Not following local laws, exploiting cheap labor, seeing Costa Rica as their personal playground, driving up costs, not trying to acclimate into the culture...

Here's a few ways to be a good expat...

Learn about the country's history and traditions. In this book, I've tried to incorporate information to help you do that but continue your research and ask locals to share stories with you.

I know I've said this before but please learn the language. You don't necessarily have to be fluent, just speak it well enough so that you can get by in most situations. Be patient with yourself as you learn. Also, don't assume that everyone will speak English.

Volunteer, participate in cultural events, and support local businesses.

Get to know the people you're buying from beyond just a simple *hola y hasta luego*.

Recently, a Tica who worked at a business that I frequented many years ago reached out to me as a mutual friend had told her that I had nearly died. She wanted to make sure I was okay. Her kind message totally made my day.

Make those types of connections. Where even if you don't see or talk to someone for an extended period of time, they still remember you fondly. And be that person for others who cross your path in life.

Prioritize experiences over material possessions. Learn how to live a simpler life. Be open-minded and flexible in adapting to the local way of life.

And lastly, while I know not everyone will agree with me, I don't recommend supporting community events that are not traditionally Costa Rican.

For example, a community-sponsored 4th of July event. It just reeks of colonization, cultural insensitivity and a disregard for the local people.

AND *gentrification.*

I recognize that Chinese New Year is celebrated in Chinatowns across the US… but this is different. We don't have "UStowns" here.

And I'm not saying that YOU can't celebrate these holidays in your home, and even invite locals to join in and learn what it means to you. But that gives Costa Ricans *a choice* versus *forcing it* on their entire town.

Don't refer to locals as "Natives"

This doesn't happen often, but I've seen people use the term, so I'm bringing it up to ensure we're all clear. Don't call local people "natives." Would you consider yourself a native of your home country? Probably not. Remember, nearly 98% of the population was originally from somewhere else.

Please be mindful of the language you use, especially when referring to the people who call our adopted home their homeland. While the term "native" may seem harmless, its implications can be loaded with colonial connotations and perpetuate a sense of otherness. Use instead: Tica, Tico or "local."

Indigenous People and Missionaries

One of the things that REALLY bothers me is when I hear about missionaries coming here to spread "the good word" amongst the Indigenous communities. It appears they realize they can no longer do it in the US so now they're branching out to other countries.

I even saw one couple who, in exchange for teaching Indigenous people about Jesus, they would help sell the arts and crafts made by the people in the community. *How about they just offer to help them sell their crafts without involving religion?*

Bringing missionary work to Indigenous people in Costa Rica disregards the cultural heritage and spiritual practices that have sustained these communities for *millennia.*

Indigenous cultures possess unique worldviews and belief systems that are deeply interconnected with their lands, languages, and traditions. *Something we could all learn from.*

Rather than imposing our values and religion, our focus should be on supporting Indigenous efforts to ensure their culture not just survives but thrives; preserving their languages and strengthening their communities. It is not just a benefit for them, but for all.

We're all "Americans"

Have you been on an international flight and had to fill out the customs paperwork and it asks: *What is your nationality?*

If you're from the US, you may have written, "American."

That term can be frustrating for people in Latin America, to the point of calling those of us from the United States, "arrogant, ignorant and entitled."

Here's why...

Latin America is part of the Americas, encompassing countries from Mexico to Argentina. So, technically, both Latin Americans and U.S. citizens are "Americans" since they are from the American continent.

The dominant language of Latin America is Spanish (*Portuguese in Brazil*), and in Spanish, people from the United States are referred to as "estadounidense". So, the use of "American" exclusively for citizens of the United States can be seen as exclusionary.

Some alternatives to consider:

- U.S. Citizen
- I'm from the US
- I'm from the States
- **And for fun**: United Statesian. Because that really is the equivalent of the Spanish term, even though it's not really a word.

While this may sound trivial to some, remember that you're no longer living in your home country. Be respectful that people here may have a different opinion – *in their home country.* Less entitlement. More humility.

It's a developing country

Since I became an entrepreneur back in 2005, my purpose, at the core of all that I do, has been to expand our worldview; encouraging us to create harmony with oneself and the world around us.

It is disheartening when I hear people use certain words that set us back decades. Two of the phrases I most dislike hearing are "third world country" and #firstworldproblems because they invoke a "them and us" mentality.

Even today, in 2024, I'm coming across people who use the term and when I try to explain what it actually means, I'm often called a crunchy granola boho hippie, or some variation of that. (*I'm actually a pragmatic hippie.*)

There Are No Third World Countries

We all live on the same planet, so there can't be three worlds.

The term dates back to a political article written in 1952 by Alfred Sauvy. In "Three worlds, one planet" published in L'Observateur he described the world as split into three political areas, each with a different role in the Cold War.

The First World was made up of U.S., Western Europe and their allies. The Second World was the Soviet Union, China, Cuba and friends, also known as the Communist Bloc. All other nations, *not assigned to either of the other two categories,* were Third World. That would include many countries like Dubai and Singapore, that we now consider to be wealthy and prosperous.

So now that I've covered the background, I think we can agree that this term, coined more than 70 years ago, is out of date.

The term preferred by many is "developing country." Whereas "third world" smacks of elitism and separation from the rest of the globe, "developing country" engenders hope and change.

Let's End First World Problems

No, I don't mean I'm here to solve your weak Wi-Fi signal or help you choose which latte you want from your local coffee shop each morning.

You're still going to have these small, minor inconveniences in your life. But please stop calling them "First World Problems."

Social media posts sporting that hashtag are like spiteful stealth boasts, screaming, "look at me, I live in one of the richest countries in the world and I've still found something (*quite trivial*) to moan about."

There's a common assumption underlying these two phrases, an assumption that is wrong — that it is better to live in a richer or developed country.

Embark on a few globetrotting adventures, or even watch a documentary from the comfort of your sofa, and you will see that quality of life is not only linked to wealth.

Some of the poorest nations on Earth boast the happiest citizens. Despite their problems, they still have a quality of life that ranks high. It may just not look like yours or mine.

Quality of life looks different in different places.

For me, this is personal. I moved to a country many people consider to be "third world."

There are bars and plywood in windows, dilapidated infrastructures, multiple families living in small homes often with dirt floors, poor nutrition, obesity, lack of good health care, homelessness, drug and alcohol problems, hunger, guns, prostitution, domestic violence, gangs, drugs, crime, murders.

Those who don't live here might judge that as "Third World," somewhere separate, a nation not as good as the "First World" countries.

But you could take that list and apply it to many places in the United States. An impressive GDP does not make a country immune to these problems.

There's no divide. If you were to look at our planet from space, you would see ONE world with no borders. Only a mosaic of colors, textures and shapes.

There is no "First World" or "Third World." Countries cannot be categorized only by their income or development or infrastructure.

There is so much more to the story. Get inquisitive, delve into a nation's culture and history, explore its landscape and you'll soon discover there is no "them and us."

We are all ONE world.

Repair, Reuse

While times are changing here and more products are becoming available in local stores, some things in Costa Rica are still either difficult to find or cost-prohibitive.

I'd invite you to, *as much as possible*, consider how you can repair and reuse products when they become broken or old.

> One of my many mantras here:
> **Do what you can with what you have.**

I have a few pairs of sandals and sneakers that I brought with me in 2012 and are still going strong... because I've taken them to the cobbler to repair again and again. Still cheaper than buying new!

I also have towels that I brought from the US. One floor towel was falling apart but rather than toss it, I found someone who could sew it and it looks like new.

When a property owner cut down a gigantic and beautiful tree in the yard, I took a piece of it to a woodworker and made an end table out of it.

Repairing and reusing items is very much a part of the culture of Costa Rica, their resourcefulness and creativity.

Instead of participating in the throwaway culture prevalent in many societies, we can learn to appreciate what we already have.

This shift in mindset encourages mindful consumption and fosters a deeper connection with the items we own.

It's illegal to remove seashells

I've mentioned other environmental laws throughout the book but as I continue to see expats asking the question, *"Where are the best seashells,"* I thought I'd include a special essay here just for that topic.

Collecting seashells often seems harmless, *"But I'm just one person taking one shell."* The reality, however, is very different. While the removal of a single shell may seem inconsequential, the collective impact of such actions can be staggering.

These shells are not mere keepsakes for our bookshelves, but rather vital pieces of coastal ecosystems, sanctuaries for countless creatures, from tiny mollusks to complex coral colonies.

With each shell taken, we chip away at the resilience of coastal habitats, leaving behind damaged ecosystems. Let us, instead, appreciate them in *their home*, untouched and unspoiled for generations to come.

It is *<u>illegal</u>* in Costa Rica to take seashells. But even if it wasn't, let us recognize our role not as masters of the Earth but rather as humble participants. Take beautiful photos, sketch or watercolor a collection of shells, but leave them behind, where they belong.

You may be wondering... *Chrissy, have you ever taken a seashell from the beach?*

Yep, I sure have. A few decades ago, before I knew it was a problem. *We don't know what we don't know... until we know it.* It's okay to make mistakes. What matters most is what you choose to do next...

And one more note: This is about more than just taking a seashell; it's about recognizing that you are one of eight billion people on this planet, and every choice you make resonates beyond the immediate moment. Your actions create ripples that can affect others both near and far, now and into the future.

The value of time (or lack thereof)

Time is highly valued in the US. Life usually revolves around the adherence to deadlines and schedules. But in other countries and cultures, the concept of time is different, more relaxed, less rigid.

"Tico Time" is something that is often joked about here, both by locals and foreigners. But for some expats, who place a strong value on time, it can lead to feelings of frustration.

So, let's zoom out and look at WHY the value of time is so very important, from a US perspective.

Part of the reason that the US is so strict when it comes to schedules and time is due to the industrial revolution. Time became synonymous with money. It's also a sign that you respect the other person or your responsibilities. And let's not forget capitalism, which emphasizes productivity, profitability and success.

On the other hand, in collectivist cultures like Costa Rica, where community harmony and relationships take precedence, *flexibility* with time may be more accepted.

While I know some business owners might disagree with me, Costa Rica is not a capitalist-driven society. It's inching its way towards being one but if you compare it to the US, the two are night and day.

Success isn't defined by how many overtime hours you spent working on a project, and "burnout" isn't a badge to wear and be proud of. I'm not even sure I've ever heard anyone here use that word!

The value of time is different here. The sooner you can accept that things don't work the same way as they might in your home country, the sooner you can experience a sense of ease from not always being in a state of "*go-go-go*."

Is your privilege showing?

Working with clients from around the world and living in Costa Rica, I have had the opportunity to know people from all walks of life.

I've known people who have had to sleep in their cars and parents who have denied themselves meals in order to feed their children. I've met people who have never left the small town where they were born, and those who have never experienced a vacation.

I have also gotten acquainted with extremely wealthy individuals, people for whom any material possession is within reach, whose every need is taken care of without question, who have traveled to all seven continents (*I know, that number is debatable*) on our planet.

Poverty and privilege, as I've learned, can take many forms.

I fall somewhere in between, in the messy middle. In Costa Rica, when I had multiple businesses, I would have been considered wealthy. Now, not so much. But I do still have a small but lovely home and a housekeeper to help with my daily to-dos.

My bank account has vacillated between abundance and scarcity, and I understand first-hand that having $13 to your name isn't a comfortable position – though certainly less dire here than in some other places in the world.

I know that I am privileged to be able to live in a beautiful place, and that my job isn't location dependent. That doesn't mean that my life is always easy or that I have a problem-free existence. It does mean, though, that I have more choices – more freedom – than a lot of other people on the planet.

My own lived experience, combined with the stories of others, has pushed me to consider the dichotomy between problems and privileges, and how sometimes the things we perceive as problems in our lives are actually a reflection of our own privilege.

I've spent a lot of time looking at my own life and recognizing *my* privilege, and the things I perceive as problems compared to the problems of those who are marginalized, underrepresented, or experiencing poverty.

I feel compelled to be more mindful about what I "complain" about and to whom.

For example, these days, I may sometimes feel stress about paying for my home and buying groceries, but it would be deeply inappropriate for me to commiserate with my housekeeper about it, when her entire income is far less than my rent.

I'd like to tell you a story.

Picture two women, both wealthy according to US standards. These are both true stories.

The first woman laments that her life is just too overwhelming. She has trouble managing her tasks – from homemade dog food to yoga to an upcoming weekend retreat with friends. She routinely fails to honor her commitments and often treats others as if their time is less valuable than her own.

The second woman comes to me and shares her own experience of feeling stressed. While she doesn't have to work and has the ability to create her own schedule, she does have a lot on her plate, and she finds it difficult to keep up with everything. After explaining her feelings, she pauses and says, *"I know these problems must seem so trivial."*

What makes her situation different from the first woman? What's the real difference between them?

It's really a matter of perspective. The first woman may be blind to – or actively avoiding the confrontation of – her privilege. Her failure to put her challenges in perspective diminishes her capacity to be compassionate to others.

She is so self-absorbed that she's lost her sense of empathy for the humans around her.

The second woman sees her own privilege with eyes wide open. She recognizes that her problems, while still impacting her own life and well-being, could be overshadowed by the problems of others in less fortunate circumstances.

Her problems are not less valid or less real than the problems of someone struggling with basic necessities, but she is able to see beyond herself and has a more expansive and understanding worldview.

The world is not binary. No one is all good or all bad – we're all works in progress. If we stay curious and open, we have a better chance of creating space for understanding and improving the world around us.

It's important to keep perspective on our unique gifts, realizing that everyone is dealing with their own challenges, some bigger and some smaller than ours.

It takes time to learn how to better manage our lives and our commitments so there is balance and harmony – so we don't drop the ball for ourselves or others – and that's okay, as long as we keep giving our best.

We're perfectly imperfect, after all.

Sometimes, all it takes to shift our perspective is a little change in the way we approach it. Here are a few ways you might realign your thinking.

Problem:
Having to set boundaries on your own work schedule
Reframe:
Some people need to work two or three jobs to make ends meet, and may have no control over their schedule.

Privilege:
Having the flexibility to work when you choose

Problem:
Struggling to choose between two equally priced homes
Reframe:
Not everyone can afford a home, or the options in their range are extremely limited or undesirable.
Privilege:
Having multiple options for where you could live

Problem:
Having trouble figuring out which sport your kid should play
Reframe:
Some families can't afford to buy both school shoes and an athletic uniform.
Privilege:
Having choices about what activities your children participate in.

Problem:
Struggling to find enough time to honor all of your social commitments
Reframe:
Some people may not have friends to spend time with, and some may have much more limited time outside of work or other commitments.
Privilege:
Having social connections and leisure time when you don't need to be working.

Perspectives on living simply (excerpt, full essay on blog!)

Here in Costa Rica, I've gained a firsthand understanding of what Gandhi meant when he said, "Live simply so that others may simply live."

When's the last time you took an inventory of your life?

Look down at your feet. Is there a floor beneath you? Is it tile, hardwood, carpet? Now consider your body. Are you healthy? Do your clothes fit, and are they clean and free of holes?

What about your home? Do the walls provide shelter from the elements? And furniture -- the table around which your family and friends gather to eat, the sofa for cuddling in front of your flat-screen TV, a memory foam mattress?

Do you have electricity? Hot and cold streaming from faucets? How about a computer? Multiple computers? Smart phones, cameras, Fitbits?

Is there food in your fridge? What will you choose to cook for dinner?

Friends, let us bathe in gratitude for everything that we have – access to education, to choices, to objects that we desire. If we're safe and we're nourished, that, in its small way, is simple luxury.

It seems so often that we -- myself included -- overlook our blessings, and continue to crave more. What we don't seem to realize is the scarcity that exists for so many, and how the way we live could impact the lives of others.

I will leave you with a challenge:

The next time you go shopping, make a different kind of list. On one side, put down what you need; on the other, note what you want.

How can you find a balance between the two? How can you shift your perspective from always wanting the next best thing and enjoy what you already have?

Perhaps you don't need to go shopping at all. Perhaps you'll realize that all you want -- and, even more, all you need -- you already have.

35

Suffrage & Beyond

Let's take a historical look back to become aware of the roles that women have played here and the challenges we still have to endure.

Suffrage, defined: From the latin word, suffragium, meaning the right to vote

The country's first steps toward suffrage coincided with other movements around the world, beginning in the late 19th century and gained momentum in Costa Rica during the 1920s and 1930s.

Despite facing resistance from traditionalists, activists persisted, organizing rallies, petitions, and educational campaigns to garner support for their cause.

In 1949, women in Costa Rica were finally granted the right to vote in national elections.

Why are women's rights lagging behind the times in Costa Rica?

- Traditional gender roles
- Machismo culture
- Education and resource gaps
- Economic disparities
- Political representation
- Cultural and social barriers
- Limited awareness and advocacy

Efforts to raise awareness and push for gender equality are ongoing. Still, a lot more work needs to be done. There is an initiative to advance the rights and equality of women by the year 2030... we'll see how far the country gets with that in the next few years.

Machismo and sexism

I've been told by a few men here that *"women shouldn't play football (soccer)."* In my mind, that is a wild – *and archaic* – statement to make. I can't get my head wrapped around it. And yes, I do ask them why and the most I get is... *"it's a man's sport."* They can't explain why other than defaulting to outdated gender roles.

While Costa Rica has made considerable progress in advancing gender equality and women's rights, deeply ingrained cultural norms and structural imbalances continue to perpetuate sexism and its detrimental effects.

I'll never forget when friends visited and asked me, *"Where are all the women?"*

That was many years ago and thankfully today, I'm seeing more women working in businesses around town, and many even have their own businesses.

But still, progress is slow in giving women the opportunities of financial independence and the freedom to be who they want to be – or even to understand that they can do something outside of the home. (*Note, not all women here face these issues!*)

Unfortunately, because machismo and misogyny are entrenched in Costa Rican society, this encourages the status quo of gender stereotypes, the "traditional" roles and behaviors that men and women are supposed to play.

I've known quite a few men here, in their 30's and 40's, who lacked even the basic skills to boil water, had never operated a washing machine, and outright refused to clean, dismissing it as "women's work."

Gender stereotypes can limit opportunities for women. Machismo continues to reinforce unequal power dynamics and systems of oppression.

Beyond women not having the same opportunities, machismo also leads to a whole lot of other problems: double standards, normalization of gender-based violence, and economic disparities.

In my research, I came across a 2022 paper by a female author from the University of Minnesota Law School, describing the inadequate laws related to gender-based violence in Costa Rica, attributing much of this to the influence of machismo. It was a disturbing read to say the least.

When women decide to seek a career, there is still a gender pay gap. A law exists for equal pay, but it exists in the US as well (*since 1963*) and women in the US are still only receiving between 78 and 84 cents for every dollar earned by their male counterpart.

Stats for Costa Rica were more difficult to confirm but it seems there was an amendment passed to the women's equality law in 2019 to ensure equal pay for women.

Recognizing that these cultural and social norms exist is the first step to understanding and challenging them.

The more we speak up, the more we serve as examples for others, and the more we can foster positive change. By standing up, we empower others to challenge traditional gender roles, helping to build a society that's more inclusive and equitable for everyone.

If we can't open our eyes to new ways of living, how will we ever progress as both individuals and collectively for the benefit of all?

How can we live in the 21st century, how can we learn that we are so much better together, that we can learn so much from each other, both men and women, *together*?

Here are five ways to help stop machismo and sexism:

If you're a woman and feel disempowered, remember that you are not defined by how society says you should be but rather who you want to be.

Throw out the status quo and know that there is another way. It might not be an easy road, but it will be worth it - *for you and for all the women and girls who come after you.*

As women, we need to start lifting each other up, honoring each other and supporting one another, especially when we ask for help. We also need to act as role models and celebrate other people's success.

If you're a man, acknowledge that it's not just your mom who should be revered but ALL women. That includes your daughters, sisters, girlfriends, wives and all the many women who you meet in a store, on the street, on a bus, wherever.

Treat them the way you treat your mother (*which is hopefully with respect, kindness and love*). And honestly, just treat everyone that way, women or men.

We ALL must be more mindful and aware of how we're showing up in our everyday lives as well as what is happening around us and out in the world. The language we're choosing to use, the people, places and events or activities we're choosing to support.

Lastly, we ALL have to keep speaking up. Pride and choosing to remain closed-minded gets us nowhere. As does fear, shame or embarrassment. We cannot remain silent on these issues. We cannot close our eyes or look the other way and ignore what is happening.

It's not going to be easy. Change is never easy. Initially, when we speak up, it may be uncomfortable, we may not be well liked but it is often the only way the tide will turn, and the story will shift.

The more we ALL contribute our voice and walk our talk, the louder, and more noticeable we will become. Together, we have influence.

Gendered language

The Spanish language, as it is today in 2024 and has been for centuries, favors men (*and forgets the women*). Here, a room of fifty women and one man would be addressed with the male pronoun.

I am fully aware that living in Costa Rica has influenced my feelings on the subject of gendered language, both in real life and online.

My eyes may have been opened a little wider because of my experiences here, and I have become more sensitive to the assumptions embedded in our everyday language.

This isn't about the Spanish language or the Latin culture, though; it's about the sneaky ways that discrimination has worked its dark magic into our way of being.

For example, in English, think about the times you've said the phrase "you guys," even though you might be speaking to a group of women.

Denying the existence of gender stereotyping only seems to perpetuate it. We need to meet it head on to break the cycle once and for all.

Check a box for "boy" or "girl"

Throughout much of the developed world, we have a history of cultivating phrases that drop us into our respective "boy" and "girl" boxes. Girls are made of sugar and spice and everything nice, boys are made of snips and snails and puppy dog tails. Boys wear blue, while pink is for girls. Even LEGO sets are separated by gender, the pink and purple of the girls' sets on a different side of the aisle from the primary colors for the boys' sets.

But these days, what qualifies as women's work? And where is this a man's world? Why is throwing like a girl associated with weakness when women are so incredibly strong? When boys will be boys, are we giving implicit permission for bad behavior or unfair treatment of others?

I was raised in the tradition of *"if you don't have anything nice to say, don't say anything at all,"* but I find that this seldom serves me – or anyone – these days, especially when so many of us don't even realize that we're using discriminatory language because it's so deeply ingrained.

It's time to speak up. Not with hatred or anger, but with curiosity and tenderness, pitching solutions instead of picking at old wounds.

It's often a difficult position to stand up and rock the boat, but I'm learning we must use our voices. We must do this for women around the world, because women and girls everywhere still face challenges every day based on their gender.

As a woman, I tend to focus more on women, but we can't ignore the fact that gender stereotypes affect men and boys, too.

They often have expectations placed on them that aren't for their benefit. How does a boy develop emotional intelligence when he grows up hearing *"boys don't cry"*? Are we teaching our boys that emotions are to be held inside or to come out in violence instead of tenderness, that being emotional equates to being womanly and therefore weak and wrong?

A Slow Shift

On a lighter note, progress is happening here in Costa Rica and in pockets around the world. For example, I'm seeing online that more and more women in Costa Rica are using the @ symbol to address both men and women in posts (as in, "amig@s" whereas traditionally it would only be *amigos*, leaving out any acknowledgement of the women, *amigas*).

Even English-speaking countries like the US have begun using "Latinx" to represent Latina/o (*and various shades in between*). This may feel like a subtle change, but it represents a major shift in thinking and serves as an indication that we're heading in the right direction.

What this is really about is the inherent balance and the harmony between the masculine and feminine in all of us, no matter where we sit along the gender spectrum.

We all have unique traits and gifts to bring to the table, and yes, there are certain tendencies associated with women and men, but in no way should we assume that all women are neat freaks who want to have a hundred babies while all men are football-loving meatheads.

Words can wound, but they can also heal us – helping us rebuild that essential yin and yang, the global community in which we will all thrive when we work together.

We can strive to stay mindful and not only listen to the words that come out of our mouths, but notice how those words affect the people around us – to adjust ourselves to be more equitable, more caring in our language.

Living here has also made me think about how the English language favors men. Even though it's not a gendered language, we do still have a natural tendency to put men first.

Boys and girls, Mr. and Mrs., brother and sister, husband and wife, male and female as well as words like congressman (congressperson), fireman (firefighter) and policeman (police officer).

You may have noticed in this book I used both the @ symbol for words like "bienvenid@" or Tic@s, as well as putting the female pronoun first.

Try it out. It might feel strange at first. But in our everyday lives, we can make small shifts to create a more inclusive, equitable and kind society.

How to be inclusive

In Spanish, as in many other languages (*French, Italian, Arabic, to name a few*), gender inclusivity is an ongoing conversation and a challenge due to its grammatical structure, which often requires gender-specific nouns and adjectives.

But you can choose to be mindful of the language you use in order to create a more welcoming environment for people of all genders in Spanish-speaking communities.

Here are a few ways to do just that:

Employ the @ Symbol or "E" Ending: Some Spanish speakers use the @ symbol (*i.e.* "tod@s" as I've done throughout the book) or add an "e" ending to words to create gender-inclusive forms. For example, instead of "amigos" (male friends) or "amigas" (female friends), you can use "amig@s" or "amigues." *While this method isn't universally accepted*, it's gaining popularity in some circles as a way to acknowledge gender diversity.

Use Collective Nouns: Instead of using gender-specific nouns, choose collective nouns that encompass all genders. For example, instead of saying "los chicos" to describe a group of girls and boys, you can say, "el grupo" (the group).

Alternate Pronouns: While Spanish traditionally uses "él" (he) and "ella" (she) pronouns, some people prefer gender-neutral pronouns like "elle" to refer to themselves. This is not widely accepted in Costa Rica (*remember I said language is very formal here*) but you can still choose to respect individuals' preferred pronouns.

Rephrase Sentences: Instead of saying "los padres" to describe a set of parents, you can say "las madres y los padres" (the mothers and the fathers), or you can say "las familias" (the families) to encompass all caregivers.

I remember the first time I saw Parents magazine in a grocery store. The title was "Padres" and I thought to myself... *Wow! They have a magazine here just for dads!*

And then a few seconds later I realized, *Oh, no, "father" is the all-encompassing word for "parents"*. Even though in all likelihood, it was the moms who were purchasing and reading the magazine. But they weren't represented in the title of the magazine.

Be an Advocate for Change: Educate others about the importance of using gender-inclusive language and encourage the adoption of more inclusive language practices in your everyday life.

Stay Informed: In 2020, the Royal Spanish Academy in Spain rejected a request to make Spanish gender neutral. But my hope is that they'll eventually revisit it. Language needs to evolve with the times. And it is time.

Heroines

Just like the Spanish language, the female heroines here are often overlooked and lesser known. If you google famous landmarks and cities named after people in Costa Rica, the overwhelming majority are all male. Of course, this doesn't just happen in Costa Rica, it's a worldwide problem.

I did my absolute best to find the most accurate information, but I found so many different stories and dates that I can't guarantee the information here is all correct.

I still feel it's worth sharing, just so you can begin to contemplate how women have helped shaped Costa Rica into what it is today.

Francisca "Pancha" Carrasco: Born in Cartago, she was a trailblazer from the start. There were no schools for girls until 1847, but Carrasco learned to read and write.

Then, as the story goes, when Costa Rican soldiers at the Battle of Rivas were in dire need of ammunition and morale, Carrasco stepped forward, distributing bullets and even taking up arms herself to fight against Walker's army, showcasing her courage and determination.

Breaking all gender roles at the time, her actions during the battle and her contribution to the war effort made her a national icon of bravery and patriotism in Costa Rica.

She was featured on a postage stamp in the 1980s, while Juan Santamaría, for the same battle, not only had a holiday designated in his honor but also an airport named after him. *I realize Santamaría died*, but maybe Carrasco could have gotten more than a stamp for her heroism.

Carmen Lyra (pen name of Maria Isabel Carvajal Quesada): Lyra was a Costa Rican writer, educator, and social activist known for her literary works that addressed social issues such as education, poverty, and women's rights. She is considered one of the most important figures in Costa Rican literature.

I came across this quote from her, and it illustrates how I previously said some people would prefer the status quo to remain intact. That some people don't want things to change.

"While I was sewing pious social patches at school and writing romantic prose with harmless metaphors for the injustice around me, I had a reputation for being an excellent person with a good heart and a 'fine' writer. But when I realized that we had to do more than trivial fixes, that we

had to fight directly against the capitalist regime, cause of the economic and social situation within which I lived; that we had to write against vested interests ... then people changed their minds about me. Now they say that I am crazy, that I am envious of the good of others, that I no longer write as before, that I have declined in the art of literature."

She was exiled to Mexico for her radical ideas and while she pleaded to return home, her request was denied.

Sor María Romero was a nun from Nicaragua who moved to Costa Rica and is remembered fondly. She was a teacher and spent much of her life helping those who were struggling, taking care of the needs of the poor, always lending a helping hand. She was known for making miracles happen.

She died in her homeland in 1977 but was buried in San José. In April 2002, Sor María Romero was beatified by Pope John Paul II, and many say she may someday receive sainthood.

Emma Gamboa Alvarado: Born in San Ramon, Gamboa Alvarado was a pioneering Costa Rican educator and women's rights advocate. She played a significant role in advancing women's access to education.

Epsy Campbell Barr: *"If we do not occupy this great avenue in which we all can recognize ourselves from our human identity, we will not achieve the dream looming on the horizon, which is the dream of dignity for all people."*

Campbell Barr is a Costa Rican politician and diplomat who became the first Afro-Costa Rican Vice-President in the country's history. She has been a leader and advocate for women's rights, racial equality, and social justice throughout her career.

So what can we do to improve the lives of women here?

As residents, we may not have a right to vote but we can still do our best to create positive change through our choices and actions. Here's an essay I wrote many years ago to inspire you to do just that.

Please Remain Standing

I have always stood up for what I believe in. Sometimes with popular opinions, sometimes against it. Sometimes with success, sometimes without.

In my teens, I protested against the closing of my high school.

In college, I protested my sorority's rush process because I refused to judge a woman's value by her appearance, declined to pay $900 in fines, and then quit the sorority (*we clearly weren't a good fit*).

In my 30's, I stood outside San Quentin State Prison at midnight on a cold December night, protesting the lethal injection of Tookie Williams. I also helped set up the protest in Oakland for the closing of the South Central Farm in Los Angeles.

Now in my 40's, one of the many things I'm doing is to create and build community rather than support the ever-growing divide. When people on either side share false facts or half-truths, I speak up. There's been a lot more of that these last few years, for sure.

My efforts haven't always created the outcomes I would've liked. But that doesn't stop me from standing up, over and over again.

Did my high school close? Yes.

Do sororities still rush girls based on their looks? Probably.

Does the death penalty still exist in California? Since 2019, there has been a moratorium.

Did the South Central Farm get paved over for a parking lot? Yes.

The outcome may not always be what you hoped for.

PLEASE REMAIN STANDING.

When you stand up for what you believe in, what you know is right, you may get screwed over, reprimanded or disparaged.

PLEASE REMAIN STANDING.

When standing you are more visible. People may judge you, dismiss you, even laugh at you. They may not fully understand your choices, your actions, your beliefs. They may even be fearful of you.

PLEASE REMAIN STANDING.

As you stand, you are respecting your own values, honoring yourself, and who you are at your very core. That, my friend, nourishes your soul.

As you stand, you may connect with new people who share similar values and beliefs, establishing a stronger network. These people will give you strength and encouragement. And together you can create a more concentrated impact out in the world.

As you stand, you will slowly but surely change the minds and attitudes of others. Your actions, your choices, will show others an alternative way to think, speak and act.

Even if you move just one person, you can make a huge impact. You've started a ripple, that will move the next person, then the next person, until the tide turns.

As you stand, more people will be encouraged to stand up for the values they believe in. And as more people stand, change will come more quickly, gathering momentum and strength, benefiting our communities, countries and planet.

We only have this one life. Wouldn't you rather choose to live it being wildhearted and outspoken than tongue-tied and wrist-bound?

We live in an imperfect world, but we can still choose to thrive, to take what is broken and do our best to repair and revive it.

Every choice you make, matters. Because change does happen. Sometimes more slowly than we'd like, but with time and perseverance change will come.

Choose to stand. Choose to honor the whisperings of your soul. Choose to make visible the values you hold so dearly. Even when it doesn't go the way you'd hoped. Even when people mock.

Doesn't that sound like a more vibrant, constructive and fulfilling way to live your one beautiful life?

Please, please remain standing.

For the single women

For some Tic@s, I am like a unicorn in Costa Rica. The surprise that occurs when I tell people that I'm single, that *yes*, I moved here on my own (*well, with my cat, and I usually say it jokingly to lighten up the conversation*) and I do not have a boyfriend or husband. Many can't understand it. Some are in awe. Some are appalled.

Thankfully, the latter mentality is changing. More local women these days are becoming financially independent, having kids later (*if at all*) and able to take care of themselves with a career and home, leading an independent and rewarding lifestyle.

One Tica hairstylist told me that her dogs were her "kids." Her mom was standing next to her, and you could tell by the look on the mom's face she wasn't exactly thrilled.

I know that transforming deeply ingrained beliefs takes time. But gender stereotypes are so last century. While progress may be slow, all around the world, gender roles are thankfully changing.

For the single women, looking for a guy

A friend once said to me... *don't get me started on all the girls who are coming here, hooking up with a local, getting pregnant and then are surprised when they find out their "amor" isn't all that he made himself out to be.*

There are some good local guys here, no doubt. But there are also a whole lot who are less than ideal.

They talk a good game and unfortunately, because of the widespread belief that everyone is friendly here, this can leave many single women vulnerable to being exploited, beyond what I already shared in The Dark Side of Paradise chapter.

See this as a forewarning and please do your due diligence. Even more so when it comes to your heart.

I have countless stories, experienced personally and shared by others, of women here facing exploitation, abuse, infidelity, manipulation, and theft, in both blatant and subtle forms.

It's hard for me to get my head wrapped around how machismo is so deeply ingrained into society here. As much as I've read and researched, it still leaves me baffled. It's 2024! Women can do more than take care of the kids, cook and clean and men can do more than go to work and light up the BBQ.

For the single women here on the Rich Coast, looking for a guy, be patient and mindful of the choices you make when it comes to meeting your *Mr. Right*.

On independence and asking for help

Contrary to what some people believe, independence is not exclusive to one gender. While our lives might not always be perfect, women can lead fulfilling and self-sustaining lifestyles.

I intentionally left out *single* before "women," because even if you're married or in a relationship, women can still be independent.

However, being independent, whatever your relationship status might be, doesn't mean never needing to ask for help.

Independence is not about isolation; it's about being self-reliant and making choices that include when to handle challenges alone and when to leverage the strengths of others. Having the confidence and courage to ask for help is not a sign of weakness, but rather strength.

Let's lift each other up, empower and support one another, regardless of gender, to create a better world, *for all*, together.

In Support of Strong Women, a poem

She stands on her own two feet.

Tired. Alone. Frustrated. Stressed. Anxious. Overwhelmed.

With heart broken open and soul aching (for more, for less, for peace).

Such a strong woman, they say, and walk away, in awe of what she has accomplished,

Blind to her invisible scars, the bruises of a life lived well and wild-hearted, the struggles she faces.

Failures, rejections, heartache.

She retreats, regroups, recovers behind the scenes as her world falls apart.

She rises up, bounding forward, supporting, stretching, giving to others even as she herself goes without.

Her mind racing, she shows up. She listens. She acts. Speaks out.

Stretches beyond herself and takes everything under the sun and stars into her arms. Touches lives.

Such a strong woman.

Behind that smile, the sparkle in her eyes, that polished, put-together, perfectly poised picture of stability, she is tired.

Spiraling. Sad. Unseen and unsupported.

She turns within.

She reaches her roots down, out, around her, solid, deep, steady, drawing strength through her body as she draws each breath into her lungs.

Patience, perseverance, passion, power.

She is bold, free, courageous.

Such a strong woman.

She may not ask for help—it's never been her strong suit. Her smile unbroken, resolve unwavering, seeking her own comfort within.

She's not alone, but she needs to know.

Do you see her? Might you be her?

Strength still needs support.

Maybe now is the time to ask.

Such a strong woman...how can I help?

36

Do You Have a Plan B?

I hope that if you decide to move to Costa Rica, and your goal is to stay here long-term, that you'll never have to implement a "Plan B."

The reality, however, is that people do move here with no intention of ever leaving, only to one day decide it's not for them.

Shifts in your life can mean uprooting and changing your location... whether it's health issues, wanting your kids to get a better education, relationship problems, financial issues, homesickness, deciding that Costa Rica isn't the right place for you, for your life, in that moment *or any number of other reasons.* No judgment here.

The unexpected can happen. A major life change can turn your life completely upside down.

Have a Plan B.

How can you prepare yourself? What will you do, where will you go, who can you turn to for support? If you don't want to return to your home country, where would you go? What are the pros and cons of the other options?

To begin, ask yourself: *"What aspects of my current situation am I most unhappy with, and how do I wish to improve them?"*

This reflection can pinpoint exactly what you're not willing to compromise on in your new environment.

Then assess what went wrong here, in Costa Rica. Did your expectations clash with reality? Were there economic or political changes? Do you need better services and resources? A different type of environment, climate or culture? A place you feel more safe?

Understanding the answers to these questions can guide you in setting clearer, more achievable goals for your move, ensuring that your Plan B addresses these issues effectively.

By focusing on what your non-negotiables are and learning from past experiences, you'll be able to make informed decisions that align with your goals and well-being in your new destination.

37

Reflections

When Harmony (my 17-year-old cat) and I arrived here in 2012, I was doe-eyed, naïve, innocent… whatever adjective you'd like to use. I've learned so much along the way. I've made more missteps, mistakes and mishaps than I care to remember.

In my book about living here, I share how I've pretty much been through it all. There was a huge learning curve and challenges like I've never experienced in California.

But I'm still here, many years later. I choose to love my life here, while acknowledging that there will always be ups and downs, twists and turns.

I've said before… *If I have to eat rice and beans every day in order to live here, I will.* I didn't actually think that would ever happen. After all, I was healthy, thriving and had multiple businesses, what could go wrong? But then it did.

After surviving severe sepsis, giving almost all the money in my bank account to the private hospital, subsequently becoming disabled, having to manage ongoing medical expenses and no longer being able to manage a full client load, *wheh*, it's been a hard road these last few years... and I found myself eating a lot of rice and beans. And peanut butter and jelly sandwiches. The former, good for healing, the latter, not so much.

People often ask me, when they hear about all the crazy stories of things that have happened along the way... *"Why are you still there??"*

The expression, *the devil you know*, often comes to mind. Of course, it's not just about already knowing how everything works, it's because I really do love Costa Rica. Even with all the challenges, it's my happy place.

So my answer is: *It's the place I get to call home. And at least for now, there's no other place I'd rather be. It isn't always easy, it's definitely not perfect, but it is so very worth it. This is where I want to be. It's a personal choice. It's my <u>home</u>.*

My hope is that this book has given you enough information to decide if Costa Rica is where you want to put down roots, for however long is right for you and your life.

I'll leave you with this poem that I wrote many years ago for myself. I've changed it to "you," so that YOU can choose how to live your ONE beautiful life.

This is your life
Your choice
Your vision
Take life off pause
Say hello to new beginnings
Goodbye to what was once
Announce buenos días to a sunrise
Buenas tardes to the sunset
And enjoy every moment in between
The howls of the monkeys
The intensity of the lapa
The quiet solitude of the sloth
The song of the toucan
The buzz of the cicada
Watching the tides roll in and out
The full moon, the new moon
The billions of stars
Fresh balmy air
Warm tropical rain
Sandy feet and blue-green waves
Surrounded by life
Take chances, let go, leap forward
Go in whichever direction life leads
Make your own path along the way
Step into your life
Live each moment with passion and purpose
Participate in this moment
leaving you breathless at the end
Make new memories
Explore, discover

The ground below, the sky above and everything in between
Create a life worth living
Live a life worth living
This is your life
Your choice
Transform
Fly free like the morpho
make your dream a reality
No hesitation
No fear

About the author

During her first trip in 2006, Chrissy Gruninger knew she'd eventually call Costa Rica home. Six years later, she packed up ten bags, her beloved cat, and bought a one-way ticket to Costa Rica, stepping into her new life, never looking back.

As an award-winning author and entrepreneur, she brings a wealth of experience and insight to her work with clients, shaped by her profound love of Costa Rica. Chrissy shares her expertise through relocation counseling and life abroad mentoring, crafted for the courageous souls whose hearts are set on calling Costa Rica "home."

Reach out to her... if you'd like to do a personalized deep dive for your move to Costa Rica, if you're already living here and need someone to talk with, to suggest feedback on this book or simply to say *hola*: costaricaexpatexpert.com/contact.